Women Empowerment through Entrepreneurship

WOMEN EMPOWERMENT THROUGH ENTREPRENEURSHIP

T. Lavanya

New Century Publications
New Delhi, India

NEW CENTURY PUBLICATIONS
4800/24, Bharat Ram Road,
Ansari Road, Daryaganj,
New Delhi – 110 002 (India)

Tel.: 011-2324 7798, 4358 7398, 6539 6605
Fax: 011-4101 7798
E-mail: indiatax@vsnl.com • info@newcenturypublications.com
www.newcenturypublications.com

Editorial office:
LG–7, Aakarshan Bhawan,
4754-57/23, Ansari Road, Daryaganj,
New Delhi – 110 002

Tel.: 011-4356 0919

Reprint: 2024

First Published: 2010

ISBN: **978-81-7708-227-2**

Published by New Century Publications and printed at Salasar Imaging Systems, New Delhi.

Designs: Patch Creative Unit, New Delhi.

PRINTED IN INDIA

About the Book

India's Eleventh Five Year Plan (2007-12) has recognized—for the first time—that women are not just as equal citizens but as agents of economic and social growth. The approach to gender equity in the Plan is based on the recognition that interventions in favour of women must be multi-pronged and they must (a) provide women with basic entitlements, (b) address the reality of globalization and its impact on women, (c) ensure an environment free from all forms of violence against women—physical, economic, social and psychological, (d) ensure the participation and adequate representation of women at the highest policy levels and (e) strengthen existing institutional mechanisms and create new ones for gender mainstreaming and effective policy implementation.

Any development strategy will be lop-sided without involving women who constitute half of the world population. Women entrepreneurship has gained momentum since the early 1980s when countries in Asia (particularly India and China) and elsewhere started liberalizing their economies. The resultant globalization propelled by foreign direct investment, technological innovations and manufactured exports has brought a wide range of economic and social opportunities to women entrepreneurs.

The present work deals with various aspects of women entrepreneurship in India. It also explains the experience of other countries in this regard.

Author's Profile

Dr. T. Lavanya is presently an Academic Consultant with the Department of Commerce and Business Management, Satavahana University, Karimnagar, Andhra Pradesh. She obtained her M.Com., LLB., M.Phil. and Ph.D. degrees from Kakatiya University, Warangal. She has been teaching for the last 8 years at under-graduate and post-graduate levels. She is a resource person for the Women Entrepreneurship Development Programmes organized in Warangal District, Andhra Pradesh.

Preface

India has committed to meeting the Millennium Development Goals (MDGs) and is a signatory to many international conventions, including Convention for Elimination of all forms of Discrimination against Women. India's Eleventh Five Year Plan (2007-12) has categorically stated that it will look at women's problems as a cross-cutting theme. It will recognize women's agency and the need for women's empowerment.

The vision of the Eleventh Plan is to end the multi-faceted exclusions and discriminations faced by women and to ensure that every woman in the country is able to develop to her full potential and share the benefits of economic growth and prosperity. The roadmap for this has already been laid in the National Policy on Women, 2001.

In the Eleventh Plan, for the first time, women are recognised not just as equal citizens but as agents of economic and social growth. The approach to gender equity is based on the recognition that interventions in favour of women must be multi-pronged and they must (i) provide women with basic entitlements, (ii) address the reality of globalization and its impact on women by prioritizing economic empowerment, (iii) ensure an environment free from all forms of violence against women—physical, economic, social and psychological, (iv) ensure the participation and adequate representation of women at the highest policy levels, particularly in Parliament and Assemblies and (v) strengthen existing institutional mechanisms and create new ones for gender mainstreaming and effective policy implementation.

The social constraints and attitudes that inhibit the development of women entrepreneurs, the atmosphere in which they work and the attitude of the society, all together have been keeping them away from the active work of entrepreneurship. The process of industrialization and urbanization has brought about socio-psychological changes in attitudes and values of people. More and more women consider self-respect and development of personality as necessary goals of life.

Women today are very much capable of running an enterprise, regardless of the hassles of life. They are equally talented as men and are satisfied and successful with their lifestyle. Entrepreneurship today does not distinguish between men and women. It calls for a stance of mind and suitable motivation, duly supported by congenial external conditions. When these are present then there emerge the central qualities of risk taking and decision-making which constitute the basis of entrepreneurship.

Any development strategy will be lop-sided without involving women who constitute half of the world population. Women entrepreneurship has gained momentum since the early 1980s when countries in Asia (particularly India and China) and elsewhere started liberalizing their economies. The resultant globalization propelled by foreign direct investment, technological innovations and manufactured exports has brought a wide range of economic and social opportunities to women entrepreneurs.

In India, development of women entrepreneurship has become an important objective of plan priorities. Several policies and programmes are being implemented—both at the levels of Central and State Governments—for the development of women entrepreneurship in India. For inclusive economic development and social justice, the socio-economic status of women in India should be improved as an overriding priority. Socio-economic freedom gives women the right to determine the course of their lives. Entrepreneurship enhances the women's social standing. The entrepreneurial activity is dependent on several complex economic, social and psychological factors. Thus, for any attempt made to understand the entrepreneurial activity among women, an analysis of their socio-economic origins is necessary.

The present work deals with various aspects of women entrepreneurship in India. It also explains the experience of other countries in this regard. Moreover, it examines in detail the activities and problems of women entrepreneurs in an important State of India, viz. Andhra Pradesh.

T. Lavanya

Contents

About the Book v
Author's Profile vi
Preface vii-ix

1. Entrepreneurship: Concepts and Dimensions **1-17**

1.1 Concept of Entrepreneurship
1.2 Entrepreneurship and Economic Development
1.3 Entrepreneurship and Social Organisation
1.4 Functions of Entrepreneurship
1.4.1 Innovation Function
1.4.2 Group Level Pattern Function
1.4.3 Leadership Function
1.4.4 Organisation Building Function
1.4.5 High Achievement Function
1.4.6 Input-completing and Gap Filling Function
1.4.7 Status Withdrawal Function
1.4.8 Social, Political and Economic Functions
1.5 Characteristics of Entrepreneurs
1.6 Entrepreneurship Development in India
1.7 Women Entrepreneurship in India
1.7.1 First Phase: 1947-83
1.7.2 Second Phase: 1983-90
1.7.3 Third Phase: 1991 Onwards
1.8 Motivation for Entrepreneurship among Women

2. Literature on Processes of Entrepreneurship Development **18-48**

2.1 Processes of Entrepreneurship Development

2.2 Entrepreneurship: General
2.3 Entrepreneurship: Characteristics and Motivation
2.4 Entrepreneurship: Selection and Training
2.5 Institutional Support for Entrepreneurship
2.6 Women Entrepreneurship
2.7 Entrepreneurship Training Programmes
2.8 Models of Entrepreneurship Development

3. Role of Women in Economic Development **49-73**
3.1 Gender and Development Approach (GAD)
3.2 Role of Gender in Economic Development
3.3 Concept and Status of Women Entrepreneurs
3.4 Strategies for Developing Women Entrepreneurship
3.5 National Policy for the Empowerment of Women, 2001
3.5.1 Objectives of the Policy
3.5.2 Politico-legal Empowerment of Women
3.5.3 Economic Empowerment of Women
3.5.4 Social Empowerment of Women
3.5.5 Operational Strategies

4. Problems of Women Entrepreneurs in India **74-81**
4.1 Barriers Faced by Women Entrepreneurs
4.1.1 Lack of Confidence
4.1.2 Lack of Working Capital
4.1.3 Socio-Cultural Barriers
4.2 Functions and Role of Women Entrepreneurs
4.3 Problems of Women Entrepreneurs
4.3.1 Financial Constraints
4.3.2 Over-dependence on Intermediaries
4.3.3 Scarcity of Raw Materials
4.3.4 Intense Competition
4.3.5 High Cost of Production
4.3.6 Low Mobility

4.3.7 Family Ties
4.3.8 Social Attitudes
4.3.9 Adverse Effects of Risk Bearing
4.3.10 Lack of Education
4.3.11 Low Need for Achievement

5. Efforts to Increase Women Entrepreneurship in India **82-96**

5.1 Role of Government
5.2 Role of Multinational Corporations (MNCs)
5.3 Role of Non-governmental Organisations (NGOs)
5.4 Micro Credit Programme
5.5 Entrepreneurship Development Programme (EDP)
5.6 Women Entrepreneurship Development (WED) Programme
5.6.1 Pre-training Stage
5.6.2 Training Stage
5.6.3 Post-training Stage
5.6.4 Awareness Building and Networking
5.6.5 Sensitization Workshops and Networking
5.6.6 Identification and Selection of Potential Women Entrepreneurs
5.6.7 Selection of Tools and Techniques
5.6.8 Curriculum Development
5.6.9 Detailed Curriculum for WED

6. Programmes and Schemes for Women Entrepreneurs **97-118**

6.1 Small Industry Development Bank of India's (SIDBI) Scheme of Assistance for Women Entrepreneurs
6.2 Bank of India's Priyadarshini Yojana
6.2.1 Scheme of Interest Subsidy for Women

Entrepreneurs
6.3 Industrial Development Bank of India's (IDBI) Mahila Udyam Nidhi (MUN) Scheme
6.4 Mahila Vikas Nidhi (MVN) Scheme
6.5 State Bank of India's (SBI) Stree Shakti Package
6.6 Eleventh Five Year Plan (2007-12) on Women Empowerment
6.6.1 Status of Women
6.6.2 Work and Employment
6.6.3 Unorganized Sector
6.6.4 Home-based Workers
6.6.5 Services Sector
6.6.6 Women in the Unorganized Sector
6.6.7 Women in Agriculture
6.6.8 Land Rights for Women
6.6.9 Impact of Globalisation and Eleventh Plan Strategy
6.6.10 Women in the Services Sector
6.6.11 Skill Development
6.6.12 Homes and Homesteads for Poor Women
6.6.13 Self-Help Groups
6.6.14 Social Empowerment
6.6.15 Political Empowerment
6.6.16 Effective Implementation of Women Related Legislations
6.6.17 Gender Mainstreaming and Strengthening Delivery Mechanisms
6.6.18 Eleventh Plan Schemes

7. Training and Motivation of Women Entrepreneurs **119-138**
7.1 Introduction
7.2 Emphasis on Women Entrepreneurship Development

7.3 Emphasis on Small Enterprise Development
7.4 Training and Motivating of Women Entrepreneurs
7.5 Inter-agency Co-operation
7.6 Effectiveness of Programmes/Courses
7.7 Methodology of Training
7.8 Motivation of Women Entrepreneurs
7.9 Identification of Potential Women Entrepreneurs
7.10 Selection of Potential Women Entrepreneurs
7.11 Guidance of Women Entrepreneurs
7.12 Adequacy of Skills to Impart Training
    7.12.1 Conceptualising Entrepreneurial and Behavioural Skills
    7.12.2 Learning and Practicing Entrepreneurial Behavioural Skills
7.13 Preparation of Feasibility Report
    7.13.1 Project Idea
    7.13.2 Techno Economic Analysis
    7.13.3 Project Design and Network Analysis
    7.13.4 Input Analysis
    7.13.5 Financial Analysis
    7.13.6 Cost Benefit Analysis
    7.13.7 Pre-investment Analysis
    7.13.8 General Information
    7.13.9 Preliminary Analysis of Alternatives
    7.13.10 Project Description
    7.13.11 Marketing Plan
    7.13.12 Capital Requirements and Costs
    7.13.13 Operating Requirements and Costs
    7.13.14 Economic Analysis
7.14 Post-training Contact of Institutions

8. Institutions Engaged in Promoting Women Entrepreneurship **139-146**
8.1 National Institute of Small Industry Extension

8.1.1 Stimulatory Activities
8.1.2 Support Functions
8.1.3 Sustaining Functions
8.2 Directorate/Commissionerate of Industries
8.3 District Industries Centre (DIC)
8.4 State Financial Corporations (SFCs)
8.5 Khadi and Village Industries Commission (KVIC)
8.5.1 Objectives of KVIC
8.6 Small Industries Service Institute (SISI)
8.7 National Small Industries Corporation (NSIC)
8.8 Small Industries Development Bank of India (SIDBI)

Appendix: Women Entrepreneurship in Andhra Pradesh: A Case Study **147-188**

Bibliography **189-204**

Index **205-214**

1

Entrepreneurship: Concepts and Dimensions

1.1 Concept of Entrepreneurship

The supplement of the Oxford English Dictionary which was published in 1933 defined entrepreneur as one who undertakes an enterprise especially contractor acting as intermediary between capital and labour. The classical economists did not attach much importance to the term entrepreneur, since they were of the opinion that under the perfect competition, the role of the entrepreneur would disappear and be changed into a sort of General Manager. Adam Smith, for instance, accorded little importance to entrepreneurship, but instead used terms such as employer, master, merchant and the undertaker. Thus, right from Adam Smith to Marshal, the study about the role and importance of entrepreneurship was not accorded due importance.

Schumpeter used the term innovation and stressed that innovation was a vital function of an entrepreneur. According to Schumpeter, the entrepreneur sees the potentiality, profitable opportunity and exploits them. Thus, according to Schumpeter, "an entrepreneur tries to maximize his profits by innovations. Innovation, in this context may refer to the introduction of new products, introduction of improved methods of production, entering new markets, locating alternative sources for raw materials and reorganization of an industrial enterprise." Entrepreneurship refers to a set of attributes which the entrepreneurs possess and a set of activities which they perform in relation to the expansion of their units. Entrepreneurship is synonymous with entrepreneurial role conformity which is to be measured in terms of entrepreneurial roles.

1.2 Entrepreneurship and Economic Development

Entrepreneurship is the driving force behind economic development. Without it, labour, capital and technology remain practically useless. Indeed, it is often not the shortage of resources, but the lack of ability and determination to put them to effective use that has retarded economic progress in the developing countries. So one of the crucial issues in planning the development of these countries is first to develop potential entrepreneurial resources and then ensure that they are employed productively.

Small enterprises provide productive outlets for the talents and energies of enterprising, independent people, many of whom would not fulfil their potential in large organisations. They provide a seedbed for entrepreneurial talent and a testing place for new industries. They enhance community stability, stimulate personal saving, promote agro-industrial linkages, improve rural welfare and generally raise the level of popular participation in the economy.

A country's economic progress is found to be positively correlated with the rise in number and quality of its entrepreneurs. Entrepreneurship has come to stay as the focal point of development. Whether it is the problem of unemployment, income generation, increasing GDP, regional imbalances in industrial progress, entrepreneurship is the potential answer.

The myth that entrepreneurs are born has been dispelled all over the world. If entrepreneurs are a class in themselves, entrepreneurship forms activities of such people. The basic objective in developing entrepreneurship and multiplying them in the society has been to enable the society generate a productive human resources, mobilize and sustain the same in subsequent process of development. The spontaneity and continuity of the process would depend on the kind of people that can be promoted and groomed in the entrepreneurial career.

It is important to harness the vigour of human potential

that convert their ideas into action can be attributed to their socio-economic values. There is no reason to believe that the population of developing countries lacks entrepreneurial talent. On the contrary, in developing countries, talented people living away from the big urban areas are not yet being absorbed by schools leading to varieties of higher-level occupations. Many able and enterprising people—among them those with entrepreneurial potential—do not find access to the proper careers and remain under-utilised in low-level employment, if they find employment at all. This applies particularly to people from the lower socio-economic strata.

1.3 Entrepreneurship and Social Organisation

Growth of entrepreneurship in a social organisation is a highly complex process. It is the result of interaction of various factors, including natural endowments, historical tradition, education and cultural standards, social stratification, religious and moral values, family organisation, social cohesion and economic development at any given period of time. Entrepreneur is among the class of leaders in a community. He undertakes a task and being associated with business environment, he sets up a business undertaking. Entrepreneur's outstanding quality is perception of business opportunity, which stems from his familiarity and deep interest in the business situation. This may be in the nature of an innovation, introducing a new product in a community or an old product in a new consumer group.

Entrepreneur belongs to the class of people who are prepared to face uncertainty and risk and take the residual income in contrast with those who, under contractual agreement, receive fixed remuneration. They get the reward in terms of profit of the business both for the capital put at risk and for the exertion as leader and organiser of the business enterprise. Further an entrepreneur is not merely an innovator because he may develop new areas, recruit and train labour, accumulate capital, reduce costs through new technology and develop new markets. Entrepreneur thus brings to bear on the enterprise a constellation of qualities for building it up and running it successfully. These qualities include initiative, innovation, decision making, capacity of hard and sustained work and ability to lead get on with people. There is however no uniform pattern of entrepreneurial behaviour for it differs from time and place within a country and within even an industrial group because an entrepreneur is a mixture of personnel traits and a myriad social and political influences and the system of values prevailing in a community to which he belongs.

1.4 Functions of Entrepreneurship

The following are the functions which are performed by entrepreneur ship, according to the various theories which have sought to explain them.

1.4.1 Innovation Function: Development is not an automatic or spontaneous process but it must be deliberately and actively promoted by some agency within the system. It is the agent which provides economic leadership that changes the initial conditions of the economy and causes discontinuous dynamic changes. He is neither a technician nor a financier, but an innovator.

1.4.2 Group Level Pattern Function: Frank W. Young was of the opinion that instead of individuals, groups with higher differentiation have the capacity to react. When a group has a higher degree of institutional land occupational diversity, relative to its acceptance, it tends to intensify its internal communication which gives rise to a unified definition of the situation. They find a way which allows mutual understanding despite the differences in the occupation and family status. Some members of the solidarity groups perform well in combining resources and emerge as entrepreneurs.

1.4.3 Leadership Function: A person who is to become an industrial entrepreneur must have additional personality traits to those resulting from drive to a mass wealth. In addition to being motivated by the expectations of profit he must also have some managerial abilities and more important, he must have the ability to lead.

1.4.4 Organisation Building Function: Entrepreneurship means the skill and ability to build an organisation. It is the organisation building skill which is considered to be the most important skill needed for the development of industrial enterprises.

1.4.5 High Achievement Function: Entrepreneurial role appears to call for the decision making under uncertainty and if the action involves applying the known and predictable techniques, the entrepreneur is not at all involved. People with high need for achievement are not influenced by monetary rewards as compared to people with low need for achievement. People with low achievement are prepared to work hard for money, while people with high achievement, and consider profit as a reward for success and competence.

1.4.6 Input-completing and Gap Filling Function: There are large gaps about the production function and it is the entrepreneurial function which fills up the deficiencies or gaps. Thus, entrepreneurs perform the function of input-completing and gap filling function. The characteristics of entrepreneurs are connection of different markets, capability of making up market deficiencies, input completing and creation and expansion of firm.

1.4.7 Status Withdrawal Function: The process of change in any society as the transition to economic growth has been aptly described by Everett Hagen. According to him, transition to economic growth has been very gradual and typically occupies a period of several generations. When members of some social group experience what he calls, 'the withdrawal of status respect', it would create response and the following four types of personalities emerge:

- Retreatist is one who continues to work, but remains indifferent to his work and position.
- Ritualist is one who adopts a defensive behaviour and acts

in the way accepted and approved in his/her society with no hopes of improving his/her position.

- Reformist is a person who inspires a rebellion and tries to establish a new order.
- Innovator is a creative individual who emerges as an entrepreneur.

1.4.8 Social, Political and Economic Functions: There is a sort of relationship between society and entrepreneurial talent; social conditions influence the stability and development of new institutions. It has been proved that for the proper development of entrepreneurship, state support is very much vital. Thus, entrepreneurship has been viewed as a function of social, political and economic structure.

1.5 Characteristics of Entrepreneurs

Entrepreneurship is a key driver of our economy. Wealth and high majority of job created by small businesses started by entrepreneurially minded individuals, many of who go on to create big businesses. People exposed to entrepreneurship frequently express they have more opportunity to exercise creative freedoms, higher self esteem, and overall greater sense of control over their own lives. As a result, many experience business people, political leaders, economists, and educators believe that fostering a rob entrepreneurial culture will maximize individual and collective economic and social success on a local, national, and global scale.

Entrepreneurs have many of the same character traits as leaders. Entrepreneurs are often contrasted with managers as administrators who are said to be more methodical and less prone to risk-taking. Some person-centric models of entrepreneurship have shown to be of questionable validity, least as many real-life entrepreneurs operate in teams rather than as single individual. David McClelland described the entrepreneur as primarily motivated by overwhelming need for achievement and strong urge to build. They are tough, pragmatic people driven by needs of independence and achievement. The entrepreneur's vision is usually supported by an interlock collection of specific ideas not available to the marketplace. The entrepreneur promotes to vision with enthusiastic passion. The entrepreneur takes the initial responsibility to cause vision to become a success. Entrepreneurs take prudent risks. They assess cost market/customer needs and persuade others to join and help.

Till the beginning of the 1990s entrepreneurship remained a topic of academic and philosophical discussion by economist, sociologist and psychologist. The attempt was to accurately define and describe entrepreneurship, its nature and functions. Such descriptions were markedly influenced by respective academic disciplines. Although most of these descriptions were partly true, yet none of them had the quality of describing entrepreneurship as a whole Moreover, such efforts lacked dynamism and devoid of action direction. These inadequacies however, led to the search for relevance and empirical support. In this process, towards the end of the 1960s, two very significant contributions were made in the field of entrepreneurship. These were:

- Establishment of positive linkage between entrepreneurship and economic prosperity; and
- Emergence of strong hypothesis that entrepreneurship can be developed through planned efforts.

The mid-seventies witnessed the crystallization of the integrated model for developing entrepreneurship consisting of stimulatory, support and sustaining activities. Training was accepted as one of the common factors to most of entrepreneurship development strategies. These were repeated and replicated in many developing countries with minor variation. Several international bodies were attracted and provide fund and experts for the implementation of the entrepreneurship development programme which were then limited primarily to the developing world. The technology and information flow was seen as the life for accelerating the process of entrepreneurship development. Towards the end of the decade, however, the unemployment problem surfaced in many developed countries. The rich experiences thus generated in developing countries were scanned and entrepreneurship development found its relevance in developed country were mobilized for refining and sharpening every aspect of entrepreneurship development strategy, through academic exercises.

The three decades of active growth has already brought adulthood to the efforts of entrepreneurship development. It has proved its usefulness and also clearly demonstrated future promises. The intervention dimensions are now, more or less clear. It has become easy for many existing or new institutions/organisations to join the main stream of organizing variety of entrepreneurship development activities. Besides, traditional EDP organizations under SME departments, many financial, educational, input related institutions and voluntary organizations have started setting up separate cells for entrepreneurship development is likely to experience significant horizontal speed. The initial emphasis on manufacturing sector is now shifting to include comparatively very wide area of service, processing, agro and rural industries on the other side.

With increasing number of entrepreneurs in the society and the organisations/institutions engaged in developing entrepreneurship, there will be general consensus among the public about entrepreneurship. This will be further accelerated by introduction of entrepreneurship as subject in school and university education system. This has already started in 80s and its impact has been visible during 1990s. The more significant impact is likely to be seen in the form of:

- Orientation to entrepreneurial career as against wage earner career.
- Increasing realization of the need of local entrepreneurs (in terms of country) with facilities for business collaboration at international level.
- Increased resentment towards regulatory and bureaucratic

functions of supporting agencies. The demand will deepen for more resulted orient procedures and facilities.

The early history of entrepreneurship development, particularly in developing world, reveals the imbalanced emphasis on stimulatory, support and sustaining activities. Usually the support activities are organized as starting point, followed by stimulatory activities. An improvement over that was the combination of stimulatory and support efforts. The anticipated consequences were the birth of large number of small business and SMEs with equally growing percentage of sickness.

The present day's strategy for developing entrepreneurship has more or less, universally accepted common frame. Very little deviation of difference is visible. It is common experiences of mid-1980s to find one or two modular strategies for entire country. This situation is likely to change during 1990s. With the increasing awareness about entrepreneurial career, the number and variety of prospective entrepreneurs will increase enormously. This will demand the variety of strategies with specialized focus. The present day models of EDPs are likely to be split. The prevalent selection procedure may lose its relevance.

Entrepreneurship development has been found a forceful movement to fight the acute problems of growing unemployment. This may generate tendency to equate entrepreneurship with self employment. All entrepreneurs are self employed, but all self employed persons are not necessarily entrepreneurs. The tendency ignore such differences may grow stronger during 1990s. This may result in dilution of EDPs and consequently may erode the credibility by producing large number of pseudo-entrepreneurs performing the task of the piece rate workers.

In order to accelerate the formulation of such new enterprises, imaginative programmes and policies, backed by sound institutional support are called for to identify, motivate and strengthen the new breed of entrepreneurs. The new entrepreneurs should come from non-traditional groups, thereby breaking the monopoly of dominant business castes and communities and diversifying the entrepreneurial resource base of the country. The programmes are also meant to make contributions towards individual growth as part of a national drive for human resource development.

1.6 Entrepreneurship Development in India

Realising this, the Government of India devised several self-employment schemes over the years to create work opportunities for these persons and groom them as risk bearing entrepreneurs. The package of assistance made available to them includes the provision of subsidy, loan on easy terms and conditions, training from specialised institutions for improvement of technical and managerial skills and entrepreneurial abilities, supply of machinery and equipment, providing raw materials etc. besides the provision of necessary information and guidance for setting up self-employed ventures.

It is a well intended movement to invigorate, rejuvenate and resuscitate the healthy and diversified socio-economic growth of the country. The development banks have expanded a network of promotional agencies at regional and state level to nourish and protect the movement with strong follow up support. The national socio economic policies and strategies are also being modified in consonance with entrepreneurship development programme. The various promotional agencies evolved and directed are acting as a friend, guide, philosopher, motivator and prime mover for new and young entrepreneurs. They are sowing the seeds of entrepreneurship promotion in every segment of the national economy. Thus, native entrepreneurship is heading towards a healthy development under the aegis, deanship, patronage and stewardship of principal development banks. The interplay of development banking and entrepreneurship promotion is getting a momentum. Thus, entrepreneurship movement is blossoming up on the crest of Indian soil. It is taking a new dimension at a time when India is actively engaged in modernising its whole economy to step in an entrepreneurial society.

The entrepreneurship movement has generated a strong unity among the entrepreneurs. The formation of 'Entrepreneurs Associations' to protect their interests and to shake-off their entrepreneurial problems and difficulties is its glaring example. The unity of purpose for bearing the attire of entrepreneurship is also on the increase. An adequate number of small and medium scale entrepreneurs associations have come into existence during the last decade. The female community has also actively come forward to participate in the entrepreneurship movement.

Entrepreneurship refers to a creative approach in business. Exploring and discovering new business opportunities, managing the enterprise excellently, taking risks and successfully introducing innovations are the entrepreneurial functions. Schumpeter regarded 'an innovation is the main feature of entrepreneurship for which profit is the reward'. At macro-level the economy of a nation depends on the availability of entrepreneurial skills. Thus entrepreneurial activity created abundant wealth and prosperity in the USA in India too it is now well realised that building up of entrepreneurial skills is a basic requirement for achieving rapid economic progress and the Government has been facilitating the development of a vigorous entrepreneurial movement in the country.

As educational facilities expand and development proceeds, the contribution that women can make also continuously rises. As the economy develops into a more industrialised one, more job opportunities get created and as the service sector expands, the opportunities for women, both in formal and informal sectors, increase still further. With further economic progress entrepreneurial opportunities are also created. In India, at present rapid progress is being witnessed and women entrepreneurship has a crucial role to play in the present environment.

1.7 Women Entrepreneurship in India

Women entrepreneurship development since independence can be analysed broadly under three phases: first phase from 1947-83, second phase from 1983-90 and third phase from 1991 onwards.

1.7.1 First Phase: 1947-83: The Government of India has taken a number of measures after independence to improve the conditions of women in general which if fully successful world have helped the creation of women entrepreneurial skills. These include the constitutional provisions, labour legislations to protect women, honouring the ILO conventions and charter that help in the field of employment, working conditions, vocational training, ensuring equal pay and helping them in the formation of women organisations and voluntary agencies that help tiny women entrepreneurs.

A pioneering step was taken during 1964-65 when the National Institute of Small Industry Extension Training (NISIET) at Hyderabad conducted an entrepreneurship development programme under the guidance of McClelland. This was followed by a scheme for technicians in 1969-70 to train the technically qualified persons and a new entrepreneurship scheme in 1971 by the Gujarat Industrial Investment Corporation. These programmes were open to all, including women entrepreneurs. Along with this, there were also attempts at organising women entrepreneurs. A significant step was taken with the declaration of the Decade for Women (1975-85) by the UN. This resulted in a series of steps to improve the status and conditions of women at all levels, including executive and entrepreneurial levels. The government, through organisations like the Small Industry Development Organisation (SIDCO), has been conducting training programmes for prospective women entrepreneurs. In 1975, the National Alliance of Young Entrepreneurs (NAYE) organised the first international conference of women entrepreneurs.

In 1978, the State Bank of India began undertaking Entrepreneurship Development Programmes (EDPs). In 1979, entrepreneurship training programmes for self-employment were arranged for the women beneficiaries of the government's TRYSEM programme. In 1981, the NAYE organised the second international conference of women entrepreneurs. The SIDO through its Small Industries Service Institutes was also organising women entrepreneurship programmes and between 1977 and 1985, it has organised, through its agencies, about 8100 training programmes in women entrepreneurship. In 1982, the government established the National Science and Technology Entrepreneurship Development Board (NSTDB) to stimulate entrepreneurship among young men and women qualified in science and technology.

Several state governments have been arranging special programmes for promoting women entrepreneurial skills in the states. Nationalised Banks and financial institutions also offer special consultancy and other assistance to women entrepreneurs and voluntary agencies working for the development of women. Since the beginning of 1980s, Employers Federation of India (EFI), Standing Conference of Public Enterprise (SCOPE) and the All India Organisation of Employers (AIOE) have been taking effective steps to promote women entrepreneurial skills.

At the time of independence, women entrepreneurs were almost a non-existent section among businessmen. However, according to 1981 Census there were 1.5 lakh self-employed women constituting 5 percent of the total self employed. Though this was not satisfactory, yet indicated the positive direction of change.

1.7.2 Second Phase: 1983-90: The year 1983 may be treated as a turning point in the entrepreneurship development since after this year it became a national movement. Two apex institutions—the NIESBUD in New Delhi and the EDII in

Ahmedabad—were established in this year. These two institutions began planning a variety of programmes for entrepreneurship, including women entrepreneurship. They also later helped in the establishment of several entrepreneurship training institutions in different part of the country. Initially there were target based programmes for different target groups like the educated, technically qualified, women, SC/ST/OBC, artisans and ex-army men. Latter, product and process-based entrepreneurship training programmes like those for plastic industry, food industry, garment industry, etc. were planned and implemented. In all such programmes, women received a significant place. For example, in 1985-86, out of a total of 1140, EDPs, women received about 10 percent (108). The NIESBUD has also brought out a training manual for trainers to be used for training different target groups.

During the latter half of 1980s several new schemes like Science and Technology Entrepreneurial Parks (STEPs), training and extension services and refinancing facilities to institutions giving financial assistance to women entrepreneurs were formulated and supported by the Industrial Development Bank of India (IDBI), which also started in 1989-90 two new programmes one called Mahila Udhyam Nidhi (MUN) under which seed capital assistance were given to women entrepreneurs and the other called Mahila Vikas Nidhi (MVN) under which NGOs dealing with women entrepreneurs were given assistance, generally one-time assistance of a capital nature. The SBI also introduced special schemes for women entrepreneurs. In 1990, the Norwegian Agency for International Development (NORAD) announced its support for entrepreneurship programme for rural poor women undertaken by government/NGOs that will ensure income generation and are replicable.

The NIESBUD decided to celebrate the year 1990 as the 25th year of Entrepreneurship Development in India. According to Akhouri of the NIESBUD, the 1980s were a decade in which entrepreneurship became a national movement. Women entrepreneurship too received its due attention in this phase. In 1986, the National Standing Committee on Women Entrepreneurs was established by the government to advice on women Entrepreneurship Development.

1.7.3 Third Phase: 1991 Onwards: The year 1991 marks an important landmark in the Indian history. In this year, the Government of India started comprehensive economic reforms by announcing changes in economic, industrial monetary, fiscal, foreign trade and foreign exchange policies. As a part of this New Economic Policy (NEP), the government also announced a special industrial policy for small scale and tiny and village industries including service units. It is estimated that early at the close of 1980s; about 50,000 potential entrepreneurs were trained in entrepreneurship including a significant section of women. As the result of the NEP, it is estimated that about 1 lakh potential entrepreneurs may be required to be trained annually. Thus, it is stated that there will be an entrepreneurial explosion in the 1990s. Many of these EDPs will have to cover weaker sections of the society. One important feature of the NEP is the revised definition of women enterprises. Earlier women enterprises were defined as enterprises where more than half of the workers/employees were women in addition to more than half of the ownership and control is by women. Under the NEP women enterprises are those where more than half of the ownership control is in the hands of women. The employment criterion has been dispensed with.

The entrepreneurship training was made more institutionalised by making it a part of curriculum in universities and other higher educational institutions especially technical and engineering institutions. For example, the SNDT women's university has been popularising entrepreneurship courses among women for over a decade. It has introduced the topic of entrepreneurship in several post-graduate courses. It has also been offering, with the UGC assistance, a number of short-term courses in entrepreneurship to its students and women in general. Special self-employment courses to rural women, through its Rural Development Centre at Udwada in Gujarat and special courses for the officials of the NGO's are also organised. Other institutions are also organising several new schemes for women entrepreneurs. The NIESBUD organised programmes for the women beneficiaries of the government's DWCRA (Development of Women and Children in Rural Areas) programmes in rural areas, especially for the Mukhya Sevikas. "Development of Micro Enterprise" programme for women have also been formulated.

Another salient feature is the special training programme for the NGOs who support women entrepreneurs. For example, the NIESBUD organised the Women's Enterprises Management Training Outreach programme (WEMTOP) in association with NGOs. For the managerial staff (called bare foot managers) or enterprises, a special programme called 'Small Enterprise Management Assistance Programme' (SEMA) has been formulated.

1.8 Motivation for Entrepreneurship among Women

Women entrepreneurs can be classified based on the different motivational criteria which inspire them to take up entrepreneurship. According to Hina Shah, women of different socio-economic and educational status opt for entrepreneurship for different reasons. Women from lower strata who are poor and less educated opt for self-employment out sheet economic necessity. Then comes, the educated and qualified who have technical knowledge but not entrepreneurial knowledge and who opt for entrepreneurship training. Then there are middle class women who have free time but have no knowledge and skills yet want to achieve something in life and hence opt for entrepreneurship. Last are the high income groups who are well off and are least interested in entrepreneurship. Women choose entrepreneurship due to: (a) economic needs, (b) the desire to satisfy personality needs (power and novel experience), (c) urge to utilise their knowledge and skills, (d) the necessity to take up family occupation, and (e) the desire to pursue entrepreneurship as a leisure time activity. It can be seen from these motivational factors that women entrepreneurship is generally perceived as a means for improving one's socio-economic status and for achieving something significant including economic independence.

2

Literature on Processes of Entrepreneurship Development

2.1 Processes of Entrepreneurship Development

Entrepreneurship is a function of at least four factors namely:

- Socio-sphere system.
- Support system.
- Resource system.
- Self-sphere system.

All the four systems interact with each other and the change in one effect in the other. Therefore, entrepreneurship may be regarded as an outcome of total interaction between these four systems.

The self-sphere system represents knowledge, skill and motivation of an individual for entrepreneurial pursuits. For an individual to emerge as a women entrepreneur, it is essential that she has knowledge of the opportunities in the environment, enterprises and technology. Further, she should have the skill to select a product or process, prepare a project report and establish an enterprise. In order to make the knowledge and skill operative, the self sphere system should have sufficient motivation, personal efficacy and coping capability.

The self-sphere system is influenced by the socio-sphere system. The behaviour of the individual is largely influenced by the family exploitation/ pressure and value orientation to independence, work initiative or innovativeness and social norms particularly with regard to risk taking. The socio sphere system constantly influences the self sphere system and the individual's behaviour takes a shape, over a period of time under the socio sphere.

Both the self-sphere and the socio-sphere are further stimulated towards entrepreneurship by the resource system available within the country. The resource system comprises of the available raw material, demand of the product, availability of technology, manpower, Power, transport, communication, market and present industries and other enterprises. This resource system which influences both the socio sphere and the self sphere, further influence the self sphere both directly and indirectly through the socio sphere and the support system.

All the three systems that is socio-sphere, self-sphere and resource system provide scope for entrepreneurship to grow under the warmth of support system. The support system mainly influences the self sphere to utilize the resource system. It has a catalytic effect and support system become operative by creating organizations and setting up organisational goals and policy conducive to the growth of entrepreneurship in the society. The support system organizes many programmes and initiates a number of activities to reach out to the members of the self sphere system. The organisational climate of the support system and the style of functioning of the members mostly decide the quality and the quantity of the outcome.

The four systems are interlinked, interact and constantly adjust to each other. Planned effort to develop entrepreneurship in a state or society requires integrated efforts covering all the four systems. Any effort to effect change in one system overlooking the other is bound to meet with failure and the overall objective to develop entrepreneurship will not be achieved. The above process of entrepreneurship development has been the base to formulate the methodology for the present study.

2.2 Entrepreneurship: General

Vinod Agarwal (1975) [1] studied the initiative, enterprise and economic choices in India. The study focuses on the past and current definitions of the entrepreneur, the various methodologies adopted for entrepreneurial studies and the history of the entrepreneur in developed and underdeveloped nations. Finally, attempts to show that in India viable patterns of entrepreneurship exist and have produced economic growth and that these patterns of entrepreneurship are sector-specific rather than national in character.

Akhouri (1974) [2] made an assessment of the performance of all six entrepreneurial motivational training centres and finally, ranks, them as per their performance. Locates the strong and weak points of the programme and suggests ways and means to overcome the present bottleneck.

James Berna (1960) [3] studied the history and present situation of 52 manufacturing firms engaged in various kinds of light engineering production in and around Madras & Coimbatore. Introduces the entrepreneurs and their background, the ways in which they have made the transition to industry, and the problems they have faced in establishing their enterprises, also evaluates their performance as industrial entrepreneurs.

Compulsky, William and Mc Nutty, Herbert (1974) [4] advocated the role of entrepreneurship in the large companies. Highlights the unique personality of the entrepreneur, the place of the entrepreneur within the social structure of big business, characteristics of the successful corporate entrepreneur, compares the small business and the large corporate bureaucracy, and the ways in which the traditional organization has been modified to allow some scope for entrepreneurship.

Inter-Institutional Group of Bihar (1974) [5] studied the Entrepreneurial talent as one of the reasons for the slow and tardy growth of industries in Bihar. It gives the details of training programme envisaged by the Inter Institutional group for Bihar for developing entrepreneurial talents.

Vinayshil Gautam (1979) [6] studied the major sectors of self-employment in this country. The role of the heritage variable in economic growth has been examined and problems of organisation structure, financial, personnel, marketing, corporate issues etc. have been highlighted with reference to entrepreneurial development.

The Committee of Development of Small and Medium Enterprises (1975) [7] constituted by the Government of India in 1973, studied the growth of entrepreneurship among new and medium entrepreneurs; existing position of facilities at the central, state and other levels; suggest measures for the enlargement and intensification of such facilities and working out a co-coordinated scheme and programme for bringing about rapid growth of new and medium entrepreneurship.

Kilby (1971) [8] studies the statements of all the major theories of entrepreneurship and a sampling of the best two empirical studies conducted in Colombia and Japan, which have attempted to apply these theories. It concludes with a modest reformulation of the entrepreneurial problem, drawing on the evidence provided in existing empirical studies of business performance in developing countries.

Patrick R. Lies (1974) [9] emphasised the seven major area of entrepreneurship, viz. searching for venture opportunities, matching an individual or team with a venture situation, evaluating the potential and long term viability of a venture, evaluating sources of finance, structuring and financing of a company carrying out negotiations and managing operations.

McClelland (1976) [10] provided a practical method of measuring of the most important human motives. It is a method, which in all probability, can be applied to other motives with equal success. Largely deals with theory of motivation achievement motive and related variables.

McClelland, DC and Winter David, G (1971) [11] attempted to check a behavioural science theory in the context of all the urgent practical problem of development institution building and provision of assistance, where and when it is required and can be financially supported.

Malgavkar (1974) [12] analysed the problem of training

for entrepreneurial development in the context of the present environment in the country, and some specific approaches to achieve the objectives of entrepreneurial development have been identified. The analysis has been illustrated by reference to field studies conducted by the SIET Institute in several states in the country.

Pathak (1975) [13] studied only small entrepreneurs, especially these registered with the State Directorate of Industries, Gujarat and their problems at various stages in the identification, crystallisation, planning and implementation of the projects. This study provides a better understanding of factors that shape an entrepreneur.

Rao and Udai Pareek (1978) [14] presents the conceptual framework and models of developing entrepreneurs. Deals with motivation, development and outlines inputs for development of skills pertaining to planning of enterprises and management. Discusses issues relating to preparatory work for entrepreneurial development programme, their follow up and support facilities to ensure better pay off.

Sharma, KL (1975) [15] present a brief historical sketch of entrepreneurial growth in India. Discusses the criteria for identification of role partners, the roles defined by them, and also identifies the entrepreneurial role patterns and the nature of their inter relationships.

Sharma, SVS (1979) [16] conducted a study based on a collaborative research project on small entrepreneurial development by seven countries viz., Bangladesh, Hong Kong, India, Korea, Malaysia, Philippines and Thailand. The report attempts to analyse the existing status and condition of small enterprises, examines the growth trends of small enterprises policies and their evaluation in regard to the promotion of small enterprises, in the participating countries. Further, it attempts to give a comparative account of policy development, programme and organisation setup with a detailed assessment of the impact of the various programmes in the participating countries. It explores the possibility of arriving at a general profile of the Asian entrepreneur on the basis of a comparative study of the profiles emerging from the individual studies. It attempts a systematic classification of the problems reported by small entrepreneurs with possible suggestions for improvement and future action.

SIET Institute (1974) [17] undertook a study which is mainly concerned with some human factors in the growth of small industry units during 1964-67 in Hyderabad and Secunderabad. It attempts to analyse empirically the biological, economical and sociological background of the entrepreneurs; the influence of psychological and sociological factors on them; the stages in the process of adoption of innovation in starting a small industry; and the influences of the environment as well as organisational assistance.

Tandon (1975) [18] analysed the factors that constitute the business environment in India for entrepreneurs. He identifies different phases of business environment, the different categories of entrepreneurs and their characteristics. The qualities of good entrepreneurs and their functions have been amply illustrated by the case studies.

Nafziger (1975) [19] study offers a perspective on vertical socio economic mobility and the difference in economic opportunities between the privileged and under privileged sections of the South Indian population. The cost and class of entrepreneur are compared to the general population, and are related to the education, experiences, internal capital and business success of entrepreneurs. 54 entrepreneurs in Vishakapatnam were interviewed in early 1971. The statistical universe consisted of 55 private indigenous industrial firms established during 1958-70 and register with the industrial department.

FASSII (1976) [20] identified the importance of encouraging entrepreneurship in backward areas and suggest some guidelines for the execution of industrial development programmes at all stages, and levels. Small industry has been recognized as an instrument to stimulate entrepreneurship. In addition, cooperation and coordination between the government and the FASII strengthening of promotional activities of SIDO programmers of intensive campaign techniques to entrepreneurship are stressed.

K.L. Sharma (1973) [21] in his article emphasized that the degree of effectiveness of these factors varies at different stages of entrepreneurial growth viz. Entry of people to manufacturing, their efforts to set up and expand business, and their sustained growth of business. Since the theoretical frame suggested here is based on the review of various studies on Indian Entrepreneurship, a more intensive empirical research is suggested to confirm its efficiency.

Singh and Kiran Kumar (1971) [22] argued that entrepreneurial behaviour is more psychological in nature than economic. They also discussed some of the factors and types of entrepreneurial behaviour.

Uplaonkar (1972) [23] in his paper explored the role of social background in influencing the growth of self-employed entrepreneurs. The specific objectives of the study are at to know whether or not self employed entrepreneurs are drawn from business or non-business background and to assess the role of business backgrounds in industrial enterprises; to explore whether or not ritual status of caste has any bearing on the choice of industry; and to find out how far educational background both liberal and technical influences the extent industrial enterprises.

Newalkar (1971) [24] studies the environment for nurturing entrepreneurial talent, even though it is not inherited. Only the right industrial environment can along nurture and nourish entrepreneurship.

. Bhat (1976) [25] suggests the inclusion of entrepreneurship development in the curriculum of diploma or degree course in two ways: as one of the subjects in the final year in the general courses and as a specialized course in entrepreneurship at the post degree level.

2.3 Entrepreneurship: Characteristics and Motivation

Gokarn (1973) [26] examined some of the shortcomings of the small scale entrepreneur and the difficulties he experiences as a result. The observations that the author makes are based on a close study of a number of small scale units and will benefit those who are already in business and those who intend to start small business of their own.

Komives (1974) [27] discussed some characteristics of an entrepreneur such as family background; early work history; schooling; nature of last employer; age at start; early company formation; risk; transactions to managership; entrepreneurial successions. Some crucial aspects in the nature of the entrepreneur are also highlighted.

Liles (1974) [28] considered the traditional thinking that entrepreneurs are special types of individuals. He states that while this may be lure for the very successful entrepreneurs, they are in most respects like many other ambitious individuals to start with.

Lift (1974) [29] identified the major structural features and contents of entrepreneurial divisions. It does this through studying some historically known entrepreneurial ventures in technology based business and industries. It suggests that the successful ventures can be distinguished from the not successful ventures in term of framework of interdependent decision.

Mandy (1973) [30] concluded that entrepreneurial competence is measured in the context of motivational variables. The measure of entrepreneurial competence was developed by factoring nine indicators of competence. It is concluded that the social and psychological skills required by entrepreneurial competence are different from those required by entry into entrepreneurial activity. The sub-cultural differences in correlates of competence were suggestive, but not significant.

Alexander (1975) [31] reviewed the change of strategies for entrepreneurship development in the last two decades. He stressed the importance of conscious efforts for facilitating entrepreneurship development in the right directions. The complex role of central and state level institutions for promoting entrepreneurship is high lighted. Points out the need for new approach to entrepreneurship development in the small scale sector in areas such as role and limitations of training in entrepreneurship; adequacy or otherwise of the institutional arrangements at the state level for promoting entrepreneurship, giving special attention to provide integrated assistance and special arrangements necessary to ensure effective co-ordination among various agencies now engaged in this programme and stimulation of local entrepreneurship in backward areas.

Nafziger (1975) [32] collected data on the distribution of entrepreneur by caste by caste and class and compared with information of the population at large, and are related to the educational attainment, occupational background, entrepreneurial and managerial experience, initial capital, access to governmental assistance, and business success of the entrepreneurs. The value added of the firm and the income class of the entrepreneur are the major indicators used for business success. These data contradict the Horatio-Alger theory of western business and economic thought, and suggests that the socio-economic class status of businessmen is substantially higher than the general population not only in India, but probably also in a large part of the rest of the non-socialist world.

Van Der Veen (1976) [33] studied the two types of entrepreneurship adopting commercial and production orientation, the former attracts many entrepreneurs because of quicker gains and more financial leverage, while the production oriented entrepreneur has to lock up his capital in fixed assets for a long term. The disadvantage of the commercial oriented entrepreneurship to developing countries is discussed. Small scale industrialists specialising in this type could reap windfall profits by disposing their import entitlements and goods. It is suggested that the Government of India take suitable steps to divert existing entrepreneurs to change their approach towards production oriented entrepreneurship.

Varadan (1971) [34] discussed the importance of small scale industry in the national economy, its development in Mysore state during the last two decade and the part played by the entrepreneurs.

Webster (1977) [35] in his article identified several types of entrepreneurs, presents a formula for classifying types of ventures appropriate for each entrepreneur and attempts to focus upon the integration of the entrepreneur and the expected type of venture, presents a conceptual model depicting the often neglected construct the independent entrepreneurial ventures.

Webster (1976) [36] introduced the concept the independent entrepreneur as a risk creator and risk avoider. The model so developed is predicted on six concepts life cycle of the firm. The rapacious act, the critical moment, the knothole.

2.4 Entrepreneurship: Selection and Training

Rondinelli & Johnson (1975) [37] in their article analyse the critical roles of decision making skills, entrepreneurial and managerial capacity at every stage of regional development with the help of a conceptual model. Identification of the functions of a planning agency in improving the desired entrepreneurial capabilities is attempted.

Timmons (1975) [38] describes and entrepreneurial development programme which addresses five fundamental aspects of entrepreneurial process; uses cases discussions, entrepreneurial simulations; self assessment exercises, group exercises and presentations, and venture analysis and business plan guidelines.

Rao (1975) [39] presents a model of entrepreneurial development. Outlines some of the findings on researches of

Indian entrepreneurs and raises several questions to set directions for future research and training for the development of entrepreneurship.

Sharma (1975) [40] highlights the programmes for development of small industries in underdeveloped areas in India and the consequent efforts as stimulation of entrepreneurship initiated from the centre as well as the state level, especially in Gujarat, Andhra Pradesh and Jammu & Kashmir. Concludes that stimulation programme has to be followed by development of entrepreneurship and that it should form part of an overall programme, if industrialisation is to become fully effective.

Venkat Rao (1975) [41] emphasises the need for developing indigenous entrepreneurship giving the examples of well known economists who recognised its importance. He highlights the multi dimensional approach to entrepreneurial development, with special reference to nature of entrepreneurial functions which are broadly classified as motivation and training, information and consultancy; and supporting facilities and services.

2.5 Institutional Support for Entrepreneurship

Chebbi (1975) [42] highlights the growing disparity between urban and rural development and attempts to show the programme by the government to correct this malady by creation of adequate infrastructure facilities in the rural areas, stimulating entrepreneurship in rural areas to create non farm employment opportunities, to increase production on farms and to take up allied activities. Reviews the strategies followed by SIET for promoting entrepreneurial talent by offering training programme, and undertaking research studies in backward areas giving an example of recent experiment conducted by the SIET in the backward state of Assam.

Patwardhan (1976) [43] describes some of the points that ought to be taken care by the entrepreneurs who want to start a small industry, such as importance of the organisational setup as well as the management information system, circumstances in which a small scale unit would fall sick and preventive measures to overcome the same, importance of proper planning, forecasting, carefully projecting the time period and the financial outlay and knowing the product and the marketing feasibility etc.

2.6 Women Entrepreneurship

Jeanne Halladay Coughlin with Andrew R. Thomas in the book "The Rise of Women Entrepreneurs- People, Processes and Global Trends" [44] documents the phenomenal growth of women-owned businesses in terms of the effects of globalisation, the issue of female equality, and the context of women's empowerment. They profile successful entrepreneurs, explaining how they got there, delineating their essential traits, and revealing what kinds of businesses they start, and categorising and explaining their economic and social motivations. The process of business formation is described along with the challenges women face and their frequently extreme solutions.

D.D. Mali in the book "Training for Entrepreneurship and Self-Employment" [45] starts with brief review of the progress made in the field of entrepreneurship development till mid 80s. Establishment of positive linkage between entrepreneurship and economic prosperity and emergence of strong planned effort was the two major contributions of 60s. Similarly varieties of EDP strategy and models were developed and field-tested during 1970s. The book concludes with points of caution against those tendencies, which are likely to dilute the EDPs efforts and consequently may erode credibility.

M.A. Khan in his book "Entrepreneurial Development Programmes in India" [46] gives an analytical account of the Entrepreneurial Development Programmes in India conducted by various promotional agencies. These agencies are playing a catalytic and crucial role in the promotion and development of small-scale entrepreneurship in different regions of the country by extending a host of supportive facilities to the potential entrepreneurs and entrepreneurs.

Narendra S. Bisht, Ramesh C. Misra and Anil K. Srivastava in their book "Entrepreneurship: Reflections and Investigation" [47] state that the problem of entrepreneurship is considered to be one of the most acute problems confronted by the under-developed economies, and the death of entrepreneurs as possibly the most potent limiting factor on their industrialisation. In our country, village and small scale industries are treated as an integral and continuing element in the economic structure. However, women entrepreneurship is an area, which has been very much neglected in academic studies and research in India.

Samiuddin in his book "Entrepreneurship Development in India" [48] states that an entrepreneur is primarily one who owns a business, has initiative and skill for production by use of an invention to produce a new product or old one in new way by new or old materials. An enterprise is an undertaking and the entrepreneur is one who organises and manages it and takes its risk. Initiative, risk bearing, co-ordinating of factors of production, use of innovation and provision of capital are the basic elements of entrepreneurship. Lack of entrepreneurship is a limiting factor for acceleration of process of industrialisation in India.

B.E.V.V.N. Murthy in his book "Entrepreneurship in Small Towns" [49] presents the story of the entrepreneurs in two small towns in coastal Andhra, who used their traditional culture and recently acquired skills to respond to new structures of economic opportunity in the process of improving their social status and initiating a process of economic change. The entrepreneurial spirit in India was displayed during pre-independence period by a few groups and sections of the society. Community-wise, Parsis and Marwaris have distinguished themselves and have set the pace for economic leadership. The history of growing entrepreneurship in India leaves many questions unanswered.

Rabindra N. Kanungo in his book "Entrepreneurship & Innovation- Models for Development" [50] focuses was on minimising the disadvantages of women by equalising educational and employment opportunities within existing development programmes. The approach was on income generation and training crafts. The assumption was that income generation would solve women's problems. Attention to the productive aspect of women's lives did not consider their reproductive roles, which do not have economic value when, performed in the family.

M. Gangadhara Rao "Entrepreneurship and Entrepreneurial Development" [51] provides a comprehensive and scintillating account of the various aspects of entrepreneurship and entrepreneurial development, outlined by distinguished academicians. The motivational dilemmas of entrepreneurs have been presented. The factors that go into successful entrepreneurship, the entrepreneurial process and promises, the problems of small-scale entrepreneurs have been discussed in an elaborate fashion subsequently.

Anupa Siddhu and others in the book "Sustainable Entrepreneurship in Communities" [52] explain that the national economy of India today is in a phase where due to globalisation, business opportunities have become extensive, so also the challenges. As a result, organisational and technological innovations, superior quality and customer satisfaction with resource optimisation would be seen as vital. Experiences of last few decades both in India and abroad clearly show that it is possible to develop entrepreneurship through planned efforts.

2.7 Entrepreneurship Training Programmes

V.R. Gaikwad, H. Gor, U. Pareek, R.V. Rao, H.C. Sah, B.G. Sah and M.C. Shetty (1974) [53] so far some 16 evaluation studies have been conducted by various organizations and individual researchers. No doubt these studies vary in their objectives, coverage and content. But one common thread in all of them is the assessment of effectiveness or impact of EDPs.

V.R. Gaikwad, H. Gor, U. Pareek, T.V. Rao, and B.G. Sah (1974) [54] the impact of EDP is measured with the help of indices relating to the entrepreneurial behaviour. The entrepreneurial behaviour is measured on the following four dimensions: Planning orientation, achievement orientation, expansion orientation and management orientation.

Patil, V.G., A. Trivedi and H.C. Rawal (1984) [55] Entrepreneurship Development organizations are lack in commitment and sincerity in conducting the EDPs. In some cases, EDPs are used as a means to generate surplus for the ED organizations.

James Curran and John Stanworth (1989) [56] there is now in a need to identify more clearly the major forms of enterprise and training education, their target populations and their resource effectiveness. 'Entrepreneurial education' or 'training for entrepreneurship' are widely used phrases, often intended to take on a generic meaning. However, most small business educational activities have little to do with promoting 'entrepreneurship' in any strict sense. In policy terms the most resource effective for currently is probably education for small business ownership but they say that the greatest need is probably for more continuing small business education although this may be expensive in resource terms.

Muthaiah and Loganathan (1990) [57] analyzed the psychosocial factors influencing entrepreneurship to evolve a strategy for selection and training of entrepreneurs based on identified attributes. The study covered 230 TRYSEM trainees of Nagpur and Aurangabad towns of Maharastra. For those who were self-employed, the support system worked well and the training institutions were also well equipped. However, they observed that the identification of trainees was not methodical and as a result 50 percent of trainees remained unemployed.

Natarajan and Jayarathram (1991) [58] suggested that

government should take various measures to develop entrepreneurship among women, such as the reorientation of educational system for women to emphasized career guidance and inclusion of entrepreneurship awareness is school curricula, providing additional concessions, giving wide publicity to such concessions, provision of facilities such as marketing support and preference in government purchases and waiving of collateral security.

Bengt Johannisson (1991) [59] Empirical research in Sweden on business venturing suggests that qualified experience and social skills are more crucial to success than formal education. Adopting an action perspective on entrepreneurship, a framework for identifying competences needed for an entrepreneurial career is provided. Entrepreneurial training calls for a contextual approach, implying, within such an entrepreneurial learning framework, different Swedish academic programmes aiming at enforcing or supplementing management skills in small firms are presented.

Suresh (1992) [60] found in his study that related to the structure of entrepreneurship in Karnataka wish special reference to small entrepreneurs in Mysore District. The following were the major conclusions of the study relating to support system in the process of industrialization: (i) due to the lethargic attitude of promotional agencies and increased incidence of sickness, the fear psychosis amongst potential entrepreneurs way very high; (ii) selection of the products was almost influenced by previous experience; (iii) the number of entrepreneurship development programmes of DIC decreased considerably over the years due to lack of adequate personnel; (iv) the single window agency was almost ineffective; and (v) the market analysis by entrepreneur was found to be non-existent and the entrepreneur relied on the information supplied by friends and well-wishers alone. The study also included the suggestion of establishing Entrepreneurship Development Institute at the state level and Industrial Data

Bank, Grievance cell and Entrepreneurship centre at the district level.

Jeffrey S. Hornsby, Douglas W. Naffziger, Donald F. Kuratko, Ray V. Montagno (1993) [61] stated that the creation of corporate entrepreneurship activity is difficult since it creates a newer and potentially more complex set of challenges on both a practical and theoretical level. On a practical level, organizations need guidelines to direct or redirect resources towards establishing effective entrepreneurial strategies.

Thomas N. Garavan, Barra O/Cinneide (1994) [62] The major problem relates to balance: too much of an emphasis on knowledge and not enough on competence; too much emphasis on information transfer learning methods and not enough on individual small group learning methods such as project teams, peer exchange, individual counselling and workshops. There is very little evaluation of the effectiveness of such programmes. There is a lack of evidence on how learning strategies influence the development of entrepreneurial competences and how these competences transfer into new project/venture formation. There is also a lack of comparative research to identify commonalities, and differences in terms of design and structure.

Verma M.K. (1996) [63] revealed that the EDPs are undertaken to serve one or more of the following objectives: (a) Accelerated industrial development by enlarging the supply for entrepreneurs, (b) Industrial development of rural and less developed areas where local entrepreneurship is not ready available and entrepreneurs from nearby cities and towns are not easily attracted, (c) Enlarging the small and medium enterprise sector which offer better potential for employment generation and wider dispersal of industrial ownership, (d) Providing productive self-employment to a number of educated and less educated young men and women leaving schools and colleges, and (e) Improving performance of small industries by supplying more selected and trained entrepreneurs, diversifying sources of entrepreneurship and therefore business ownership.

Saini J.S. and B.S. Bhatia (1996) [64] determined the effectiveness of EDPs through a comparative analysis of performance by trained and untrained entrepreneurs was undertaken in Northern India. The findings of the study reveal that trained and untrained entrepreneurs had no significant difference in terms of availing facilities and incentives, time taken in project implementation, capital investment per person employed, sales turnover achieved per person employed, capital efficiency achieved, time taken in achieving break-even level of sales and growth rate of capital investment. However, retrained entrepreneurs showed significantly higher growth rate of employment and sales. Also the trained entrepreneurs were better than untrained ones in terms of entrepreneurial vision and future plans. Entrepreneurial talent exists in every society and in all cross-sections of people.

Briga Hynes (1996) [65] Entrepreneurs or the move towards self employment is, and will continue to become, an increasingly important element of economic growth and development. It is now recognized that small firms in Ireland are "net creators of jobs while the large firm sector is a net shedder of jobs". To ensure that a sustained increase in self-employment continues, it is critical that the correct infrastructure is in place to facilitate this development. One critical aspect of this infrastructure is the creation of an enterprise culture which will encourage and entice individuals to take the risk of starting a business. Focuses on how a process model for enterprise education can be sued to target various student groups in an interdisciplinary manner, and emphasizes the need to teach entrepreneurship to non-business student, who in many instances are the originators of ideas, but unfortunately do not have the business knowledge to develop the idea further.

Ranade (1996) [66] pointed out that rate of success was reduced not due to entrepreneurial inadequacy but because of business environmental deficiencies. He concluded that the

EDP models were to be more dynamic, flexible, market based to meet the requirements of different economic strata, social strata and infrastructure strata existing in the country.

Dinesh N., Awasthi and Jose Sebastian (1996) [67] the performance of EDPs across the states and across the ed organizations have not been uniform the actual start up rates are observed to be oscillating between 9 percent and 56 percent, bringing down the over all national start up rate to about 26 percent which cannot be consider as impressive performance. And in this non impressive performance lies the need for looking at the problems and the constraints of EDPs.

Rathore, S., D.D. Sharma and S.K. Dhameja (1998) [68] Majority of the respondents were diploma holders followed by graduate engineers and other technical entrepreneurs. Since diploma holders in engineering are found more suitable for entrepreneurship, certain specific schemes may be launched to further encourage this group of the technical entrepreneurs to come forward for establishing their ventures. The technical entrepreneurs are advised to undergo a comprehensive EDP before venturing into an entrepreneurial career.

Prabath (1998) [69] emphasized on the induction of new approaches to meet the emerging needs of the twenty first century's entrepreneur. The hypotheses put to test were: (i) the need for achievement is essential for entrepreneurial success and (ii) achievement motivation can be developed. The six experimental training programmes on achievement motivation conducted by McClelland's model were adopted. The effect of the behavioural training on entrepreneurial activity was assessed in comparison with control groups. Results revealed that those who participated in the courses showed more active business behaviour, worked longer hours, made more definite attempts to start new business ventures and actually started more such ventures. They also made specific investment in new fixed productive capital and employed more workers. The trained entrepreneurs showed larger percentage increases in their gross income and demonstrated increased entrepreneurial activity. It was suggested to review the existing methods of training and skills and introduce new approaches for entrepreneurship development during the next century. These experimental programmes emphasized the positive relationship between 'Need for Achievement' and entrepreneurship.

P.N. Ram (1998) [70] revealed that in order to achieve dispersed growth of small scale industries in view of their appreciable contribution to employment generation, regional development and economic growth, a significant importance was attached to entrepreneurship development from non-traditional communities right from the beginning of our planning. It has been experienced that non-traditional class of entrepreneurs do not respond spontaneously to available business opportunities despite various incentives and concessions due to lack of entrepreneurial talent.

Akhouri (1999) [71] analyzed the progress made in the field of entrepreneurship development during 1990s. The major contributions of the 1960s were the establishment of positive linkage between entrepreneurship and economic prosperity and the emergence of strong planed effort. In 1970s a variety of EDP strategy and models were developed. During 1990s, there was a shift from generalist to extension specialist approach and development of more precise EDP strategies. He concluded that all entrepreneurs were self-employed, but all self employed persons were not necessarily entrepreneurs. He observed that this might result in dilution of EDPs and consequently might erode the credibility by producing large number of Pseudo-entrepreneurs performing the task of the piece rate workers.

According to Sarah L. Jack, Alistair R. Anderson (1999) [72] the enterprise culture is founded on the premise that entrepreneurship is the engine that drives the economy. One aspects of this cultural pervasion is the increase in the numbers of educational institutions teaching entrepreneurship courses. Yet this hegemony of the encouragement of new business start-up, almost for its own sake, needs to be critically reviewed. Graduating enterprise students must be innovative and creative to satisfy the need for entrepreneurial novelty – the art. Yet, paradoxically they also need to be competent and multifunctional managers.

Kulakarni (1999) [73] concluded that entrepreneurship development received considerably emphasis from the 1970s beginning with the Fourth Plan and implemented effectively to motivate and stimulate the educated unemployed in particular, potential investors among the rural rich, non-resident Indians, scientists, technologists, engineers etc. According to him, the overall strategy for the development of village and small industries broadly comprised of: (i) integration of promotional programmes for the sector with other areas of development programmes which could also correct the regional imbalance; (ii) organization of production and distribution functions with deliberate bias towards village small industry sector in such a way as to create opportunities for filler and additional employment on dispersed and decentralized basis and (iii) creation of suitable organizational base at various levels to implement the development programmes for the sector. Some other notable support measures for the small enterprises included: reservation of items for exclusive production and purchase; provision of financial and fiscal incentives supply of raw materials and machinery through small industries through the wide network of promotional bodies, viz. Small Industries Service Institute (SISIs); District Industries Centres (DICs); Central Institute of Tool Design (CITD); Institute for Design and of Electrical Measuring Instruments (IDEMI) and National Institute for Entrepreneurship and Small Business Development (NIESBUD). The success of EDPs, conceived as an integral part of promotional agencies, would mean faster growth of small enterprises run by young and highly motivated entrepreneurs.

Dhana. L.P. (2001) [74] Entrepreneurship create wealth and reduces unemployment. Entrepreneurs contribute to industrialisation as well as to economic growth; they improve living standards and tax revenues from their enterprises contribute to a nation's treasury. Not surprisingly, then, governments have been spending considerable sums trying to create entrepreneurs. The question remains, however, Can entrepreneurship really be taught? To provide a response of any value, one must address the definition of entrepreneurship. As evident from the literature, there is no universally accepted definition of entrepreneurs or of entrepreneurship. If entrepreneurship is equated with the causing of economic disequilibrium—as per the Schumpeterian literature—than one can argue that entrepreneurs tend to be born, rather than made. In contrast, if relying on the definition provided by the Austrian School of Economics, it is possible to train entrepreneurs to identify opportunities and act thereon. Thus, while it can be argued that it is difficult to teach Schumpeterian entrepreneurship, efforts to teach Kirznerian entrepreneurship appear to have achieved some levels of success. However, to be truly successful, training programmes must be relevant to the host environment. It would be a fallacy to assume that a programme that has been functional in one environment will necessarily have the same effect elsewhere.

Neal E. Thornberry (2003) [75] Large organizations that had embarked on formalized "corporate entrepreneurship" management development programs formed the basis for this field research. Results indicate that many managers can indeed be trained to act like entrepreneurs and that these actions can result in significant new value creation. However, companies who embark on corporate entrepreneurial development programs also need to be award of the pitfalls and problems that can happen, when newly trained corporate entrepreneurs re-enter the organization.

Kuratko, Donald F. (2005) [76] Entrepreneurship has emerged over the last two decades as arguably the most potent economic force the world has ever experienced. With that expansion has come a similar increase in the field of entrepreneurship education. The recent growth and development in the curricula and programs devoted to entrepreneurship and new-venture creation have been remarkable. The number of colleges and universities that offer courses related to entrepreneurship has grown from a handful in the 1970s to over 1,600 in 2005. Some legitimacy has been attained in the current state of entrepreneurship education; there are critical challenges that lie ahead.

2.8 Models of Entrepreneurship Development

In the background of emphasis of emphasis on managerial strategies, several researchers have developed the models for entrepreneurship development. A brief explanation of these models has been presented below.

Amostuck School of Business Management (1969) [77] presented a model, which envisaged the growth of entrepreneurship in Manufacturing units in many stages viz. (i) perception of opportunities to set up a unit, (ii) idea projection, (iii) assembling usable power, (iv) creation of an organization i.e. transfer of organizational decision making from one person or group of persons to another and (v) adaptive organization, i.e. adjusting the organisation to the existing milieu after it has been properly routed. It proposed to study the effect of ethnic group, caste, class, social values, national goals and public policies at different stages.

Rao (1975) [78] advocated a five stage entrepreneurial training mode. First was the 'Stimulation Stage', which included the creation of industrial atmosphere, policy statements on the role of small entrepreneurs, announcement of special schemes and creation of support system. The second was the 'Identification State' within which prospective entrepreneurs in various groups' namely rural artisans, factory workers, persons who had formal training in technical areas and the graduates in business administration and management are identified. The third stage being 'Development and Administration' covered motivation and managerial training programmes to help in venture initiation. Forth stage was

'Promotion State' and it consisted of establishment of various supporting institutions to arrange necessary developmental facilities, services and generates more useful strategies with a view to effectively implement them.

Akhouri (1980) [79] suggested the following activities for the promotion and development of entrepreneurship; i. Stimulatory, ii. Support and iii. Sustaining activities. The stimulatory activity referred to all such activities that stimulate entrepreneurship in any society. The support activity referred to all such activities that helped entrepreneurs in establishing and running their enterprise and the sustaining activities to those that helped in continued efficient and profitable functioning of an enterprise.

Srivatsava (1988) [80] visualized two stages for entrepreneurship development model viz. horizontal model and vertical model. The horizontal model suggests the setting up of a central agency. The District Entrepreneurial Centre, to make a comprehensive study of business potentials of that area. This agency would also make an estimate of financial and institutional requirements of prospective entrepreneurs.

Sadhak (1989) [81] forward a Resource Linked Integrated Mode. The contention of this model was that while initiating entrepreneurship development, local conditions like socio-economic situation, local social, political and economic institution, locally available manpower and above all, natural resources should be taken into account so that the trained entrepreneurs would be capable of exploiting local resources. He also suggested that separate EDP institutes for backward and non-backward areas should be developed.

The model conceptualized by Sahney (1989) [82] related to women entrepreneurship development. He observed that women possessed many traits required for entrepreneurial success, like sense of responsibility, devotion of duty, sincerity of purpose, determination and capability of hard work, what they lack is the opportunity.

Akhouri and Mishra (1990) [83] suggested that

entrepreneurial education should become a part of school curriculum so that entrepreneurial culture, including values, attitudes, motivation and competencies could be infused among the people at an early stage in their lives and suggested a two-stage model. In the early stage of education, the entrepreneurship education containing more inputs related to entrepreneurial spirit, comparatively moderate inputs of motivation and very little inputs for competencies in the beginning years of school life should be given to germinate entrepreneurial culture. In the higher secondary stage, the maximum inputs related to competencies might be offered, followed by moderate stressing on motivation and comparatively much less coverage of entrepreneurial spirit.

There is little evidence of empirical research available to show the role of stimulatory, support and sustaining functions in the promotion of women entrepreneurship and the entrepreneurial attitude orientation behavioural tendencies among women entrepreneurs. The aim of the present research is to work on the gap in the literature. Hence, it is justified to carry out an in-depth study, and research on the Motivational Climate of Organisations (MCO), Clientele Satisfaction and Entrepreneurial Attitude Orientation of Women Entrepreneurs.

Notes

1. Vinod K. Agarwal (1975), Initiative Enterprise and Economic choices in India: A Study of the Patterns of Entrepreneurship, Munshiram Manoharlal.
2. Akhouri, MMP (1974), Evaluation of Entrepreneurial Motivation Training Programme in Assam, SIET Institute, Hyderabad.
3. Jams J Berna (1960),Industrial Entrepreneurship in Madras State, Asia publishing House.
4. William Copulasky and McNutty, Herbert (1974), Entrepreneurship and the Corporation, New York.
5. Inter-Institutional Group of Bihar (1974), Entrepreneurial Development Programme for Bihar, Patna.
6. Vinayshil Gautam (1979), Enterprise and Society: A Study of Some aspects of Entrepreneurship and Management in India,

Concept Publishing.
7. Ministry of Industrial Development (1975), Report of the Committee on Development of Small and Medium Entrepreneurs, India Investment Centre.
8. Kilby (1971), Entrepreneurship and Economic Development, Free Press, New York.
9. Patrick R. Liles (1974), New Business Venture and Entrepreneur, Richard D. Irwin.
10. McClelland, D.C. (1976), Achievement Motive, Irving Publishers, New York.
11. McClelland, DC and Winter David G (1971), Motivating Economic Achievement, Free Press, New York.
12. Malgarkar P.D. (1974), Training for Entrepreneurial Development; Review and Approach, Occasional Paper No.51 Training Division, Dept. of Personnel and Administrative Reform, New Delhi.
13. Pathak H.N. (1975), Problems of Small Scale Entrepreneurs: Report on a Study Based in Gujarat, Industrial Development Bank of India.
14. Rao T.V., Udai Pareek (1978), Developing Entrepreneurship; A Handbook of Learning Systems, Delhi.
15. Sharma K.L. (1975), Entrepreneurial Performance in Role Perspective, Abhinav Publications, New Delhi.
16. Sharma SVS (1979), Small Entrepreneurial Development in Some Asian Countries, Light and Life publishers, New Delhi.
17. SIET (1974) Socio-Psychological Factors Influencing the Adoption of the Innovation of Starting a Small Industry Unit: A Research Study, SIET Institute, Hyderabad.
18. Tandon (1975), Environment and Entrepreneur, Chug Publication.
19. Nafziger (1975), Entrepreneurship in India, Political Science Quarterly, LXXX (4), P.558-573.
20. FASSII (1976), Growth of Entrepreneurship in Backward Areas, FASII Bulletin, 15(5) 7-8 &12.
21. K.L. Sharma (1973), Growth of Small-scale Entrepreneurship in India; Theoretical Frame of Analysis, inter discipline 1973, (3), 7-108.
22. Singh, NP and Kiran Kumar (1971), Motivational Structure Underlying Entrepreneurship Behaviourometric, 1(2), 89-98.
23. Uplonkar (1972), A study of self-employed industrial

entrepreneurs, the Indian Journal of Social Work, 1977, 38(2), 137-147.

24. Newalker (1971), Creating environment for entrepreneurship, productivity, 1971, 12(1), 35-38.
25. Bhat (1976), Entrepreneurship in Curricular of Engineering Studies, Young Alliance, 8 (9), 19-21.
26. Gokarn (1973), The making of successful small scale entrepreneur, Indian Manager, 4 (1), 51-58.
27. Konives (1974), What are Entrepreneurs Made of? Chemical technology, 4(12), 716-721.
28. Liles (1974), Who are the entrepreneurs? MSU Business Topics, 22(1), 5-14.
29. Lift (1974), Why Entrepreneurs succeed, Journal of General management, 1(2), 77-93.
30. Mandy (1973), Motives, Modernity and Entrepreneurial Competence, Journal of Social Psychology, 1973, 91(I Half) 127-136.
31. Alexander (1975), Entrepreneurship Development: Need for a Pragmatic Approach, SEDME, 2(1), 1-8
32. Nafziger (1975), Class, Caste and Community of South Indian Industrialists: An examination of Horatio-Alger Model, the Journal of development studies, 11(2), 131-148.
33. Van Der Veen (1976), Commercial Orientation of Industrial Entrepreneurs in India, Economic and Political Weekly, 11 (35), M.91-94.
34. Vardan (1971), Development of Ancillaries and Entrepreneurial Skills, Integrated Managements, 61, 10-14.
35. Webster (1977), Entrepreneurs and Ventures: An attempt at classification and clarification. Academy of Management review, 2(1), 54-61.
36. Webster (1976), Model for new ventures initiation a discourage on capacity and the independent entrepreneur, Academy of Management Review 1(1), 26-37.
37. Rondinelli and Johnson (1975), Decision Making Managerial capacity and Development: An entrepreneurial approach to planning, African Administrative Studies, (13), 105-118.
38. Timmons (1975), Guided Entrepreneurship, Business, Horizons, 18(6), 49-52.
39. Rao T.V. (1975), Development of an entrepreneur: A Behaviouristic model, SEDME, 1(4), 325-343.

40. Sharma (1975), Stimulation of Entrepreneurship in less developed areas, some Indian experiences, SEDME, 1(4), 345-363.
41. Venkat Rao (1975), A multi dimensional approach to development of entrepreneurship: Significance of training and other inputs, SEDME, 1(4), 285-300.
42. Chebbi (1975) V.K, Stimulating rural entrepreneurial initiatives, SEDME, 2(i), 59-72.
43. Patwardhan (1976), What banks expect from the Small Scale Industries, Industrial Times, 18(8), 27-31.
44. Jeanne Hallday Coughlin and Andrew R. Thomas, The Rise of Women Entrepreneurs, People, processes, and Global trends, Published by Quorum Books, West Port London. ISBN-1-56720-462-7 (2002).
45. D.D. Mali, Training for Entrepreneurship and Self Employment, Mittal Publications, New Delhi, ISBN-81-7099-667-8.
46. M.A. Khan (1992), Entrepreneurial Development Programmes in India, Kanishka Publishing House, New Delhi
47. Narendra S. Bisht, Ramesh C. Misra and Anil K. Srivastava (1989), Entrepreneurship Reflections and investigations, Published by Chugh Publications, Allahabad.
48. Samiuddin (1989), Entrepreneurship Development in India, Mittal Publications, New Delhi
49. B.E.V.N.N. Murthy (1989), Entrepreneurship in Small Towns, Mittal Publications
50. Rabindra N. Kanungo (1998), Entrepreneurship and Innovation Models for development, Sage Publications, New Delhi
51. M. Gangadhara Rao (1992), Entrepreneurship and Entrepreneurial Development, Kanishka Publishing House, New Delhi.
52. Anupa Siddhu, Sustainable Entrepreneurship in Communities, Published by Academic Excellence, New Delhi.
53. Gaikwad, V.R (1974), Entrepreneurship Development Programmes: An Evaluation, Indian Institute of Management, Ahmedabad.
54. Gaikwad, V.R. (1974), An interview schedule to measure Entrepreneurial Behaviours, 11 M, Ahmedabad.
55. Patil, V.G., A. Trivedi and H.C. Rawal (1984), How to successfully fail in EDPs, Occasional Papers, entrepreneurship Development institute of India, Ahmedabad.

56. James Curran and John Stanworth (1989), Education and training for enterprise: Problems of classification, Evaluation, Policy and research, International Small Business Journal, Sage Publications, Vol.7, No.2, p.11-22.
57. Muthaiah, B.C. and M. Loganathan (1990), Psychosocial Factors influencing Entrepreneurship in Rural Areas, Journal of Rural Development, Vol.9, No.1, pp.237-38.
58. Natarajan. K and M. Jayarathnam (1991), Entrepreneurship: A Means to Women Development, Khadi Gramodyog, Vol.37, No.12, pp. 357-360.
59. Bengt. Johannison (1991), University Training for Entrepreneurship: Swedish Approaches, Vaxjo University, Sweden Entrepreneurship & Regional Development, Volume.3, Issue-1, January, Pages 67-82.
60. Suresh, B.H. (1992), Industrial Entrepreneurship in Karnataka– A Case Study of Small Scale Industrial Units in Mysore District, Unpublished Ph.D. thesis submitted to university of Mysore.
61. Jeffrey. S. Hornsby, Douglas W. Naffizer, Donald, F. Kuratko, and Ray V. Montagno (1993), An Interactive Model of the Corporate Entrepreneurship Process, Journal Entrepreneurship: Theory and Practice, Vol.17.
62. Thomas N. Garavan and Barra O'Cinneide (1994), Entrepreneurship Education and Training Programme. A Review and Evaluation – Part-I, Journal of European Industrial Training, MCB UP Ltd., Vol.18, Issue: 8, Page: 3-12.
63. Verma M.K. (1996), Government-Industry Partnership, EDII, Ahmedabad.
64. Saini J.S., and B.S. Bhatia (1996), Impact of Entrepreneurship Development programmes, Journal of Entrepreneurship Development, pp.23-27.
65. Briga Hynes (1996), Entrepreneurship Education and Training Introducing Entrepreneurship into Non-Business Disciplines, Journal of European Industrial Training, MCB UP Ltd. Vol: 20, Issue:8, Page. 10-17.
66. Ronade. S.P. (1996), Entrepreneurship Development Model for 21st Century: A Short Note, SEDME, Vol. XXIII, No.2, PP.47-48.
67. Dinesh N. Awasthi and Jose Sebastian (1996), Idib.p.116.
68. Rathore, B.S., D.D. Sharma and S.K. Dhanuja (1998), Impact of Various Schemes on Technical Entrepreneurs in Hariyano, HRD

Times.

69. Prabath S.V. (1996), Entrepreneurship Development in India: A Review, SEDME, Vol. XXX, No.3, pp.1-5
70. Ram P.N. (1998), Entrepreneurship in Education Main Stream, The Hindu.
71. Akohouri MMP (1999), Training for Entrepreneurship and Self Employment, New Delhi, Mittal Publications, pp.1-12.
72. Sarah L. Jack, Alistair. R, Anderson (1999), Entrepreneurship Education within the Enterprise Culture: Producing Reflective Practitioners, International journal of Entrepreneurial Behaviour 7 Research, 125, McB UP Ltd., Vol : 5, Issue: 3 p.110.
73. Kulakarni, P.R. (1999), Entrepreneurship Development: Role of the Government and Institutional Agencies, Southern Economist, Vol.38, No.8, pp.12-14.
74. Dhana, L.P.(2001), The Education and Training of Entrepreneurs in Asia, Education Training, Emerald Group Publishing Limited, Vol. 43, Nov. 8, 2001, pp. 405-416 (12)
75. Neal, E., Thornberry (2003), Corporate Entrepreneurship : Teaching Managers to be Entrepreneurs, Journal of Management Development, MCB UP Ltd. Vol.22, Issue:4, Page 329-344.
76. Kuratko, Donald. F (2005), The Emergence of Entrepreneurship Education: Development, Trends and Challenges, Entrepreneurship Theory and Practice, Blackwell, Publishing, Vol.29, No.5, Sept. 2005, pp.577-598 (22)
77. Anostuck School of Business Management Seminar on Entrepreneurship, Working Papers and Project Proposal for an Entrepreneurial Process, Dartmoth College, 1969.
78. Rao. B.S.V. (1975), A Multi Dimensional Approach to Entrepreneurship Significance of Training and Other Inputs" SEDME, Vol.1, No.4, pp.75-87.
79. Akhori M.M.P., Self Employment through Entrepreneurship Development Strategies
80. Srivastava. A.K., R.C. Mishra and N.S. Bisht (1988), Developing Entrepreneurship: A Strategic Layout, Man and Development, SEDME, Vol.10, No.3, pp.117-124.
81. Sadhad. H (1989), The Role of Entrepreneur in Backward Area, New Delhi: Daya Publishing House.
82. Sahney. M (1989), Women Entrepreneurship, Financial Express, Oct. 14, p.7.
83. Akhouri M.M.P. and S.P. Mishra (1980), Entrepreneurship

Education: A Conceptual Base, Approach and Methodology, Indian Management, 1990, Vol.29, Nos. 11 & 12, pp.53-65.

3

Role of Women in Economic Development

Entrepreneurship is the foundation of a new model of development for developing countries. It has been widely recognized that traditional strategies for aiding the third world have produced mixed results, with the failure of many modernization programs linked to factors such as tensions with indigenous cultural values, difficulty in maintaining capital intensive initiatives and adverse effects of large scale development projects on the natural environment. In a newer, more grassroots approach, the focus is on enabling the poor to improve their lives by obtaining the necessary training to successful launch their own small business (micro enterprises), including the acquisition of small business acumen and micro-entrepreneurial skills. Such skills are often addressed in development projects through consulting and technical assistance by NGOs who also frequently assist with the acquisition of the necessary capital through various microfinance strategies. These small ventures can be easier to sustain because of their strong links to local people, less capital intensive scale and greater environmental sensitivity.

3.1 Gender and Development Approach (GAD)

In the 1980s, the Gender and Development Approach (GAD) influenced by social feminism, post-modern and post-colonial theories, took into account the totality of women's lives, rejecting the public/private dichotomy which serves to devalue women's work at home. Focus on women's perspectives on development make women the 'subjects' rather than 'objects' of development, change agents rather than welfare recipients. The GAD approach is to move women from the margin to the centre by women gaining a sense of control over their lives (empowerment).

Entrepreneurship activities for women are clearly within the GAD framework. Development cannot be sustained unless the people for whom it is intended are at the centre of development activity. Emphasis on economic development without attention to quality of life has resulted in uneven economic growth but not development of societies. The goal of development is not merely to initiate a process of economic growth but also a process which will improve the lives of people. This implies improvement in the quality of lives of all segments of the population, particularly those groups which have been traditionally marginalized, such as women. Demographic variables are affected directly or indirectly by the status of women within the family and in society, in particular their educational level and economic involvement.

It is not always easy for women to find a job that will be suitable with their family responsibilities and household chores. Thus, many women are attracted by the idea of self-employment in enterprises adjoining their house premises with flexible hours which allows them to take care of both home and business. Small-scale enterprises represent an important means of earning income for women in developing countries. They provide employment and income to alleviate poverty conditions.

In India, the Planning Commission, central and state governments recognize that women should be in the mainstream of economic development. In particular, the development of micro enterprises for women is seen as an appropriate way to attack poverty at the grass roots level by generating income. Industrial policy of the Government of India has highlighted the need for entrepreneurship programmes for women to enable them to start small scale enterprises.

Despite the efforts of governmental and non-governmental organisations the number of women entrepreneurs is very small. Several factors explain this. There is a great deal of research concerned with gender differences in motives for starting micro enterprises, and in the attitudes and strategies related to their survival and growth.

First, enterprises always involve risk-taking. For women, gender stereotyped perception of self, lack of confidence and assertiveness pose barriers to risk taking. Fear of non-traditional and outside the home activities prevent risky ventures. Second, heavy domestic commitments and resistance of social structure to change also pose problems. The status of women in a patriarchal social structure makes women dependent on the males in their lives–husband or father–and family resistance is a major disincentive to start-up. Also, other family members often make decisions for women. Third, lack of access to education and training for women is another problem. Finally, obtaining finances, even small amounts, is an uphill task for women. The lack of collateral perceptions of women's ability is contrary to the experience of organizations – women have been consistently found to be effective in the utilization of credit and subsequent repayment of loan. Also, women's savings are found to be twice as much as that of men.

Yet, male bias in training courses and assistance programmes designed for and by mean continues and, male imagery and vocabulary, and policies and technology targeted at men continue. Women are more isolated socially, lack previous work experience (a factor in business success), and access to enterprise information and marketing facilities. Because of women's position within the family and structure of power relations, it is important to get husband's/father's support within the GAD framework. Positioning may facilitate ability to call upon a wide range of family support. The 'politics of location' is something that women in India have always understood.

However, merely dumping resources into women's programmes will not solve the problem of women's employment. Many schemes fail to provide women with income as well as opportunities which are sustainable. Income generating projects often fail because products cannot be sold, or because women do not know the economics of what they are doing. Women need training in functional areas such as finance, marketing, production and managerial skills. Women's involvement in cooperatives requires literacy and education. Illiterate women are shy to join organizations. The need is to focus on women's educational opportunities. To become entrepreneurs in single or cooperative firms, women first need to understand their own capabilities and possibilities.

Women and men employ different strategies which are motivated by their very different circumstances. Male-owned enterprises usually grow vertically, whereas women tend to grow by diversifying into other activities. Women are less concerned with making money. They see the enterprise as a means of simultaneously meeting career needs and childcare role. What they earn is totally spent for the benefit of the entire family. Another key motivating force for women to become business owners has been identified as interest in helping others.

After economic liberalization of 1991, India is passing through a decisive stage of socio-economic development. An increase in entrepreneurial activity is playing a major role in this development. It is believed that the existing latent entrepreneurial talents, if properly harnessed, could help in fostering the pace of socio-economic development, balanced regional growth, exploring locally available resources and creating gainful employment and self-employment. In developing countries including India, favourable socio-economic environment helps in exploiting the latent entrepreneurial talents of women, and unfavourable situations hinder the emergence of entrepreneurial talent. Despite situational constraints in India, more and more women are entering into the field of entrepreneurship.

The rationale behind women becoming economic actors has been examined by various researchers. The Report of the

National Commission on Self-employed Women and women in informal sector suggests that self-employment is not the only way women can express themselves economically. While women possessing skills, education, and a sense of enterprise may be encouraged to take up self-employment, those from the poorer sections who possess neither the skills nor the desire for self-employment need to be provided with wage employment.

Women are culturally well equipped to run their own business, due to skills developed through managing households, raising children etc. Therefore, a shift from family management to enterprise management may be easier than a shift from paid employment to self-employment.

Women who try to enter an industry, either in a managerial or in an entrepreneurial role are generally exposed to various environmental constraints. Starting a business or operating a business involves considerable risk and effort on the part of an entrepreneur. Developing entrepreneurial capability and putting it into optimum use are major problems faced by a majority of women entrepreneurs.

Entrepreneurship Development Programme (EDP) sensitizes the potential entrepreneurs to establish their own benchmark in the industrial activity in a planned manner. Entrepreneurship denotes the spirit of enterprise and initiative in creation of something of value against any odds that may come on the way. Entrepreneurship is the process of creating something of value by devoting the necessary time and effort and assuming the accompanying financial, psychological and social risks for great personal satisfaction. Risk taking appears to be one of the several personality traits of an entrepreneur. EDP emphasis practical hands on experience. It is designed to motivate the participant, guide them in the selection of appropriate opportunities and develop their managerial skills.

3.2 Role of Gender in Economic Development

The role of gender in economic development processes has been increasingly recognized as crucial, both in terms of the potential for success and the nature of the impact of particular development strategies and programs. Gender becomes especially important to consider when the grassroots, micro-enterprise approach is considered, as the traditional home-cantered roles of women can make it far easier for women to participate in such programs, as opposed to the more-traditional, large scale, top down programs.

Due to the prescribed social roles for women that centre on their position in the home, small enterprises that incorporate the home can empower women, Gender-based theories of the economy have long recognized that social advancement and independence for women is strongly related to women's ability to both earn and control income. We can thus expect economic empowerment to be linked to social empowerment. Studies have also shown that initiatives that enhance women's access to and control of income enhance the welfare of their children, especially in the areas of education and health, more than when men earn and/or control income. Not only is this important for children's welfare, but since improving the health and education of children is crucial for the long term economic development of the society. It is also important for the whole society's prospects for advancement.

3.3 Concept and Status of Women Entrepreneurs

Women entrepreneurs may be defined as the women or a group of women who initiate, organize and operate a business enterprise women are expected to innovate, imitate or adopt an economic activity to be called "women entrepreneurs". The Government of India has defined a woman entrepreneur as "an enterprise owned and controlled by a woman having a minimum financial interest of 51 percent of the capital and giving at least 51 percent of the employment generated in the enterprise to women." However, this definition has come in for severe criticism on the condition of employing more than 50 percent women workers. The critics point out that this is discriminatory and any enterprise set-up by women should qualify for the concessions offered to women entrepreneurs.

Since the 21st Century, the status of women in India has been changing a result to growing industrialization and urbanization, spasmodic mobility and social legislation. Over the years, more and more women are going in for higher education, technical and professional education and their proportion in the workforce has also been increased.

With the spread of education and awareness, women have shifted from the kitchen, handicrafts and traditional cottage industries to non-traditional higher levels of activities. Even the government has laid special emphasis on the need for conducting special entrepreneurial training programmes for women and enable them to start their own ventures. Financial institutions and banks have also set up special cells to assist women entrepreneurs. This has boomerang the women entrepreneurs on the economic sense in the recent years although many women's entrepreneurship enterprises are still remained in a much neglected field.

However, for women there are several handicaps to enter into and manage business ownership due to the deeply embedded traditional mindset and stringent values of the Indian Society.

3.4 Strategies for Developing Women Entrepreneurship

Following strategies can be adopted for effective development of women entrepreneurship.

1. Consider women as specific target group for all developmental programmes.
2. Better educational facilities and schemes should be extended to womenfolk
3. Adequate training programmes on management skills to be provided to women.
4. Encourage women's participation in decision-making.
5. Vocational training to be extended to women community that enables them to production process and production management.

6. Skill development to be done in women's polytechnics and Industrial Training Institution to work in training-cum-production workshops.
7. Training on professional competence and leadership skill to be extended to women.
8. Training and counselling on a large scale of existing women entrepreneurs to reduce lack of self-confidence and fear of success.
9. Counselling through the aid of committed NGOs, psychologists, managerial experts personnel should be provided to existing and emerging women entrepreneurs.
10. Continuous monitoring and improvement of training programmes.
11. Activities in which women are trained should focus on their marketability and
12. Making provision of marketing and sales assistance from government part.
13. To encourage more passive women entrepreneurs the women training programmes organised that taught to recognize her own psychological needs and express them.
14. State Finance Corporations and financing institutions should permit by stature to related finance to women entrepreneurs.
15. The financial institutions should provide more working capital assistance both for venture and large scale ventures.
16. Making provision of micro credit system and enterprise credit system to the women at local level.
17. Repeated gender sensitization programmes should be held to train financiers to dignity and respect as persons in their own right.
18. Infrastructure, in the form of industrial plots and sheds, to set up industries is to state run agencies.
19. Industrial estates could also provide marketing outlets for the display and sale exhibitions.
20. A women entrepreneur's guidance cell is set up to handle the various problems of women entrepreneurs all over the

state.

21. District Industries Centres and Single Window Agencies should make use of all their trade and business guidance.
22. Programmes for encouraging entrepreneurship among women are to be extended.
23. Training to entrepreneurial attitudes should start at the high school level through courses, which build confidence through behavioural games.
24. More governmental schemes to motivate women entrepreneurs to engage in small business ventures.
25. Involvement of Non Governmental organisations in women entrepreneurial training and counselling.

Independence brought promise of equality of opportunity in all sphere to the Indian woman guaranteeing for their equal rights of participation in political process and equal opportunity in education and employment where enacted. But unfortunately, the government sponsored development activities that have benefited only a small section of women. The large number may still remain unaffected by chance and development.

3.5 National Policy for the Empowerment of Women, 2001

The National Policy for Empowerment of Women 2001 was formulated for bringing about advancement, development and empowerment of women in all spheres of life through creation of a more responsive judicial and legal system sensitive to women and mainstreaming a gender perspective in the development process. The strengthening and formation of relevant institutional mechanisms and implementation of international obligations/commitments and co-operation at the international, regional and sub-regional level was another commitment.

The principle of gender equality is enshrined in the Indian Constitution in its Preamble, Fundamental Rights, Fundamental Duties and Directive Principles. The Constitution not only grants equality to women, but also empowers the

State to adopt measures of positive discrimination in favour of women.

Since Independence in 1947, there has been a marked shift in the approach to women's issues from welfare to development. Within the framework of a democratic polity, India's laws, development policies, schemes/programmes under Five Year Plans have aimed at women's advancement in different spheres. In recent years, the empowerment of women has been recognized as the central issue in determining the status of women. The National Commission for Women was set up by an Act of Parliament in 1990 to safeguard the rights and legal entitlements of women. The 73rd and 74th Amendments to the Constitution of India provided for reservation of seats in the local bodies of Panchayats and Municipalities for women, laying a strong foundation for their participation in decision making at the local levels.

India has also ratified various international conventions and human rights instruments committing to secure equal rights of women. Key among them is the ratification of the Convention on Elimination of All Forms of Discrimination against Women (CEDAW) in 1993.

The Mexico Plan of Action (1975), the Nairobi Forward Looking Strategies (1985), the Beijing Declaration as well as the Platform for Action (1995) and the Outcome Document adopted by the UNGA Session on Gender Equality and Development & Peace for the 21st century, titled "Further actions and initiatives to implement the Beijing Declaration and the Platform for Action" have been unreservedly endorsed by India for appropriate follow up.

The women's movement and a wide-spread network of Non-government Organisations (NGOs) which have strong grass-roots presence and deep insight into women's concerns, have contributed in inspiring initiatives for the empowerment of women.

However, there still exists a wide gap between the goals enunciated in the Constitution, legislation, policies, plans, programmes, and related mechanisms on the one hand and the situational reality of the status of women in India, on the other.

Gender disparity manifests itself in various forms, the most obvious being the trend of continuously declining female ratio in the population in the last few decades. Social stereotyping and violence at the domestic and societal levels are some of the other manifestations. Discrimination against girl children, adolescent girls and women persists in parts of the country.

The underlying causes of gender inequality are related to social and economic structure, which is based on informal and formal norms, and practices.

Consequently, the access of women – particularly those belonging to weaker sections including Scheduled Castes/Scheduled Tribes/Other backward Classes and minorities, majority of whom are in the rural areas and in the informal, unorganized sector – to education, health and productive resources, among others, is inadequate. Therefore, they remain largely marginalized, poor and socially excluded.

3.5.1 Objectives of the Policy: The primary objective of the policy was to bring about the advancement, development and empowerment of women. Specifically, the objectives of this Policy included the following:

1. Creating an environment through positive economic and social policies for full development of women to enable them to realize their full potential
2. The *de jure* and *de facto* enjoyment of all human rights and fundamental freedom by women on equal basis with men in all spheres – political, economic, social, cultural and civil
3. Equal access to participation and decision making of women in social, political and economic life of the nation
4. Equal access to women to health care, quality education at all levels, career and vocational guidance, employment, equal remuneration, occupational health and safety, social security and public office etc.

5. Strengthening legal systems aimed at elimination of all forms of discrimination against women
6. Changing societal attitudes and community practices by active participation and involvement of both men and women.
7. Mainstreaming a gender perspective in the development process.
8. Elimination of discrimination and all forms of violence against women and the girl child; and
9. Building and strengthening partnerships with civil society, particularly women's organizations.

3.5.2 Politico-legal Empowerment of Women: Legal-judicial system would be made more responsive and gender sensitive to women's needs, especially in cases of domestic violence and personal assault. New laws would be enacted and existing laws reviewed to ensure that justice is quick and the punishment meted out to the culprits is commensurate with the severity of the offence.

At the initiative of and with the full participation of all stakeholders including community and religious leaders, the Policy would aim to encourage changes in personal laws such as those related to marriage, divorce, maintenance and guardianship so as to eliminate discrimination against women.

The evolution of property rights in a patriarchal system has contributed to the subordinate status of women. The Policy would aim to encourage changes in laws relating to ownership of property and inheritance by evolving consensus in order to make them gender just.

Women's equality in power sharing and active participation in decision making, including decision making in political process at all levels would be ensured for the achievement of the goals of empowerment. All measures would be taken to guarantee women equal access to and full participation in decision making bodies at every level, including the legislative, executive, judicial, corporate, statutory bodies, as also the advisory commissions, committees, boards, trusts etc. Affirmative action such as reservations/quotas, including in higher legislative bodies, will be considered whenever necessary on a time-bound basis. Women–friendly personnel policies will also be drawn up to encourage women to participate effectively in the developmental process.

Policies, programmes and systems would be established to ensure mainstreaming of women's perspectives in all developmental processes, as catalysts, participants and recipients. Wherever there are gaps in policies and programmes, women-specific interventions would be undertaken to bridge these. Coordinating and monitoring mechanisms will also be devised to assess, from time to time, the progress of such mainstreaming mechanisms. Women's issues and concerns as a result will specially be addressed and reflected in all concerned laws, sectoral policies, plans and programmes of action.

3.5.3 Economic Empowerment of Women: Since women comprise the majority of the population below the poverty line and are very often in situations of extreme poverty, given the harsh realities of intra-household and social discrimination, macro economic policies and poverty eradication programmes will specifically address the needs and problems of such women. There would be improved implementation of programmes which are already women oriented with special targets for women. Steps would be taken for mobilization of poor women and convergence of services, by offering them a range of economic and social options, along with necessary support measures to enhance their capabilities.

In order to enhance women's access to credit for consumption and production, the establishment of new, and strengthening of existing micro-credit mechanisms and micro-finance institution would be undertaken so that the outreach of credit is enhanced. Other supportive measures would be taken to ensure adequate flow of credit through extant financial institutions and banks, so that all women below poverty line have easy access to credit.

1. Women's perspectives would be included in designing and implementing macro-economic and social policies by institutionalizing their participation in such processes. Their contribution to socio-economic development as producers and workers would be recognized in the formal and informal sectors (including home based workers) and appropriate policies relating to employment and to her working conditions would be drawn up.

Globalization has presented new challenges for the realization of the goal of women's equality, the gender impact of which has not been systematically evaluated fully. It is evident that there is a need for re-framing policies for access to employment and quality of employment. Benefits of the growing global economy have been unevenly distributed leading to wider economic disparities, the feminization of poverty, increased gender inequality through often deteriorating working conditions and unsafe working environment especially in the informal economy and rural areas. Strategies would be designed to enhance the capacity of women and empower them to meet the negative social and economic impacts, which may flow from the globalization process.

In view of the critical role of women in the agriculture and allied sectors, as producers, concentrated efforts would be made to ensure that benefits of training, extension and various programmes would reach them in proportion to their numbers. The programmes for training women in soil conservation, social forestry, dairy development and other occupations allied to agriculture like horticulture, livestock including small animal husbandry, poultry, fisheries etc. would be expanded to benefit women workers in the agriculture sector.

The important role played by women in electronics, information technology and food processing and agro industry and textiles has been crucial to the development of these sectors. They would be given comprehensive support in terms of labour legislation, social security and other support services to participate in various industrial sectors.

Women at present cannot work in night shift in factories even if they wish to. Suitable measures will be taken to enable women to work on the night shift in factories. This will be accompanied with support services for security, transportation etc. The provision of support services for women, like child care facilities, including crèches at work places and educational institutions, homes for the aged and the disabled would be expanded and improved to create an enabling environment and to ensure their full cooperation in social, political and economic life. Women-friendly personnel policies would also be drawn up to encourage women to participate effectively in the developmental process.

3.5.4 Social Empowerment of Women: Equal access to education for women and girls would be ensured. Special measures would be taken to eliminate discrimination, universalize education, eradicate illiteracy, create a gender-sensitive educational system, increase enrolment and retention rates of girls and improve the quality of education to facilitate life-long learning as well as development of occupation/vocation/technical skills by women. Reducing the gender gap in secondary and higher education would be a focus area. Sectoral time targets in existing policies would be achieved, with a special focus on girls and women, particularly those belonging to weaker sections including the Scheduled Castes/Scheduled Tribes/Other Backward Classes/Minorities. Gender sensitive curricula would be developed at all levels of educational system in order to address sex stereotyping as one of the causes of gender discrimination.

A holistic approach to women's health which includes both nutrition and health services would be adopted and special attention would be given to the needs of women and the girl at all stages of the life cycle. The reduction of infant mortality and maternal mortality, which are sensitive indicators of human development, is a priority concern. The

Policy reiterated the national demographic goals for Infant Mortality Rate (IMR), Maternal Mortality Rate (MMR) set out in the National Population Policy 2000. Women should have access to comprehensive, affordable and quality health care. Measures would be adopted that take into account the reproductive rights of women to enable them to exercise informed choices, their vulnerability to sexual and health problems together with endemic, infectious and communicable diseases such as malaria, TB, and water borne diseases as well as hypertension and cardio-pulmonary diseases. The social, developmental and health consequences of HIV/AIDS and other sexually transmitted diseases would be tackled from a gender perspective.

To effectively meet problems of infant and maternal mortality, and early marriage the availability of good and accurate data at micro level on deaths, birth and marriages is required. Strict implementation of registration of births and deaths would be ensured and registration of marriages would be made compulsory.

In accordance with the commitment of the National Population Policy (2000) to population stabilization, this Policy recognizes the critical need of men and women to have access to safe, effective and affordable methods of family planning of their choice and the need to suitably address the issues of early marriages and spacing of children. Interventions such as spread of education, compulsory registration of marriage and special programmes like BSY should impact on delaying the age of marriage so that by 2010 child marriages are eliminated.

Women's traditional knowledge about health care and nutrition would be recognized through proper documentation and its use will be encouraged. The use of Indian and alternative systems of medicine would be enhanced within the framework of overall health infrastructure available for women.

In view of the high risk of malnutrition and disease that

women face at all the three critical stages viz., infancy and childhood, adolescent and reproductive phase, focussed attention would be paid to meeting the nutritional needs of women at all stages of the life cycle. This is also important in view of the critical link between the health of adolescent girls, pregnant and lactating women with the health of infant and young children. Special efforts would be made to tackle the problem of macro and micro nutrient deficiencies especially amongst pregnant and lactating women as it leads to various diseases and disabilities.

Intra-household discrimination in nutritional matters vis-à-vis girls and women would be sought to be ended through appropriate strategies. Widespread use of nutrition education would be made to address the issues of intra-household imbalances in nutrition and the special needs of pregnant and lactating women. Women's participation would also be ensured in the planning, superintendence and delivery of the system.

Special attention will be given to the needs of women in the provision of safe drinking water, sewage disposal, toilet facilities and sanitation within accessible reach of households, especially in rural areas and urban slums. Women's participation would be ensured in the planning, delivery and maintenance of such services.

Women's perspectives would be included in housing policies, planning of housing colonies and provision of shelter both in rural and urban areas. Special attention would be given for providing adequate and safe housing and accommodation for women including single women, heads of households, working women, students, apprentices and trainees.

Women would be involved and their perspectives reflected in the policies and programmes for environment, conservation and restoration. Considering the impact of environmental factors on their livelihoods, women's participation will be ensured in the conservation of the environment and control of environmental degradation. The vast majority of rural women still depend on the locally available non-commercial sources of energy such as animal dung, crop waste and fuel wood. In order to ensure the efficient use of these energy resources in an environmental friendly manner, the Policy would aim at promoting the programmes of non-conventional energy resources. Women would be involved in spreading the use of solar energy, biogas, smokeless chulahs and other rural application so as to have a visible impact of these measures in influencing eco system and in changing the life styles of rural women.

Programmes would be strengthened to bring about a greater involvement of women in science and technology. These would include measures to motivate girls to take up science and technology for higher education and also ensure that development projects with scientific and technical inputs involve women fully. Efforts to develop a scientific temper and awareness will also be stepped up. Special measures would be taken for their training in areas where they have special skills like communication and information technology. Efforts to develop appropriate technologies suited to women's needs as well as to reduce their drudgery would be given a special focus too.

In recognition of the diversity of women's situations and in acknowledgement of the needs of specially disadvantaged groups, measures and programmes would be undertaken to provide them with special assistance. These groups include women in extreme poverty, destitute women, women in conflict situations, women affected by natural calamities, women in less developed regions, the disabled widows, elderly women, single women in difficult circumstances, women heading households, those displaced from employment, migrants, women who are victims of marital violence, deserted women and prostitutes etc.

All forms of violence against women, physical and mental, whether at domestic or societal levels, including those arising from customs, traditions or accepted practices shall be dealt with effectively with a view to eliminate its incidence. Institutions and mechanisms/schemes for assistance will be created and strengthened for prevention of such violence, including sexual harassment at work place and customs like dowry; for the rehabilitation of the victims of violence and for taking effective action against the perpetrators of such violence. A special emphasis would also be laid on programmes and measures to deal with trafficking in women and girls.

All forms of discrimination against the girl child and violation of her rights shall be eliminated by undertaking strong measures both preventive and punitive within and outside the family. These would relate specifically to strict enforcement of laws against prenatal sex selection and the practices of female foeticide, female infanticide, child marriage, child abuse and child prostitution etc. Removal of discrimination in the treatment of the girl child within the family and outside and projection of a positive image of the girl child would be actively fostered. There would be special emphasis on the needs of the girl child and earmarking of substantial investments in the areas relating to food and nutrition, health and education, and in vocational education. In implementing programmes for eliminating child labour, there would be a special focus on girl children.

Media would be used to portray images consistent with human dignity of girls and women. The Policy would specifically strive to remove demeaning, degrading and negative conventional stereotypical images of women and violence against women. Private sector partners and media networks would be involved at all levels to ensure equal access for women particularly in the area of information and communication technologies. The media would be encouraged to develop codes of conduct, professional guidelines and other self-regulatory mechanisms to remove gender stereotypes and promote balanced portrayals of women and men.

3.5.5 Operational Strategies: All Central and State

Ministries would draw up time bound Action Plans for translating the Policy into a set of concrete actions, through a participatory process of consultation with Centre/State Departments of Women and Child Development and National /State Commissions for Women. The Plans would specifically include the following:

1. Measurable goals to be achieved by 2010.
2. Identification and commitment of resources.
3. Responsibilities for implementation of action points.
4. Structures and mechanisms to ensure efficient monitoring, review and gender impact assessment of action points and policies.
5. Introduction of a gender perspective in the budgeting process.

In order to support better planning and programme formulation and adequate allocation of resources, Gender Development Indices (GDI) would be developed by networking with specialized agencies. These could be analyzed and studied in depth. Gender auditing and development of evaluation mechanisms would also be undertaken along side.

Collection of gender disaggregated data by all primary data collecting agencies of the Central and State Governments as well as Research and Academic Institutions in the Public and Private Sectors would be undertaken. Data and information gaps in vital areas reflecting the status of women will be sought to be filled in by these immediately. All Ministries/Corporations/Banks and financial institutions etc would be advised to collect, collate, disseminate and maintain/publish data related to programmes and benefits on a gender disaggregated basis. This would help in meaningful planning and evaluation of policies.

Institutional mechanisms, to promote the advancement of women, which exist at the Central and State levels, will be strengthened. These would be through interventions as may be appropriate and would relate to, among others, provision of adequate resources, training and skills to effectively influence macro-policies, legislation, programmes etc. to achieve the empowerment of women.

National and State Councils would be formed to oversee the operationalisation of the Policy on a regular basis. The National Council would be headed by the Prime Minister and the State Councils by the Chief Ministers and would be broad in composition having representatives from the concerned Departments/Ministries, National and State Commissions for Women, Social Welfare Boards, representatives of Non-Government Organizations, Women's Organisations, Corporate Sector, Trade Unions, financing institutions, academics, experts and social activists etc. These bodies would review the progress made in implementing the Policy twice a year. The National Development Council would also be informed of the progress of the programme undertaken under the policy from time to time for advice and comments.

National and State Resource Centres on women would be established with mandates for collection and dissemination of information, undertaking research work, conducting surveys, implementing training and awareness generation programmes, etc. These Centres would link up with Women's Studies Centres and other research and academic institutions through suitable information networking systems.

While institutions at the district level would be strengthened, at the grass-roots, women would be helped by Government through its programmes to organize and strengthen into Self-Help Groups (SHGs) at the Anganwadi/Village/Town level. The women's groups would be helped to institutionalize themselves into registered societies and to federate at the Panchyat/Municipal level. These societies would bring about synergistic implementation of all the social and economic development programmes by drawing resources made available through Government and Non-Government channels, including banks and financial institutions and by establishing a close Interface with the Panchayats/ Municipalities.

Availability of adequate financial, human and market resources to implement the Policy would be managed by concerned Departments, financial credit institutions and banks, private sector, civil society and other connected institutions. This process would include the following:

1. Assessment of benefits flowing to women and resource allocation to the programmes relating to them through an exercise of gender budgeting. Appropriate changes in policies will be made to optimize benefits to women under these schemes;
2. Adequate resource allocation to develop and promote the policy outlined earlier based on (1) above by concerned Departments.
3. Developing synergy between personnel of Health, Rural Development, Education and Women & Child Development Department at field level and other village level functionaries'
4. Meeting credit needs by banks and financial credit institutions through suitable policy initiatives and development of new institutions in coordination with the Department of Women & Child Development.

The strategy of Women's Component Plan adopted in the Ninth Plan of ensuring that not less than 30 percent of benefits/funds flow to women from all Ministries and Departments will be implemented effectively so that the needs and interests of women and girls are addressed by all concerned sectors. The Department of Women and Child Development being the nodal Ministry will monitor and review the progress of the implementation of the Component Plan from time to time, in terms of both quality and quantity in collaboration with the Planning Commission.

Efforts would be made to channelize private sector investments too, to support programmes and projects for advancement of women

The existing legislative structure would be reviewed and additional legislative measures taken by identified departments to implement the Policy. This would also involve a review of all existing laws including personal, customary and tribal laws, subordinate legislation, related rules as well as executive and administrative regulations to eliminate all gender discriminatory references. The process would be planned over a time period 2000-03. The specific measures required would be evolved through a consultation process involving civil society, National Commission for Women and Department of Women and Child Development. In appropriate cases the consultation process would be widened to include other stakeholders too.

Effective implementation of legislation would be promoted by involving civil society and community. Appropriate changes in legislation would be undertaken, if necessary.

In addition, following other specific measures would be taken to implement the legislation effectively.

1. Strict enforcement of all relevant legal provisions and speedy redressal of grievances would be ensured, with a special focus on violence and gender related atrocities.
2. Measures to prevent and punish sexual harassment at the place of work, protection for women workers in the organized/ unorganized sector and strict enforcement of relevant laws such as Equal Remuneration Act and Minimum Wages Act will be undertaken,
3. Crimes against women, their incidence, prevention, investigation, detection and prosecution would be regularly reviewed at all Crime Review fora and Conferences at the Central, State and District levels. Recognised, local, voluntary organizations would be authorized to lodge Complaints and facilitate registration, investigations and legal proceedings related to violence and atrocities against girls and women.
4. Women's Cells in Police Stations, Women Police Stations, Family Courts, Mahila Courts, Counselling Centres, Legal Aid Centres and Nyaya Panchayats would be strengthened

and expanded to eliminate violence and atrocities against women.

5. Widespread dissemination of information on all aspects of legal rights, human rights and other entitlements of women, through specially designed legal literacy programmes and rights information programmes would be done.

Training of personnel of executive, legislative and judicial wings of the State, with a special focus on policy and programme framers, implementation and development agencies, law enforcement machinery and the judiciary, as well as non-governmental organizations would be undertaken. Other measures would include the following:

1. Promoting societal awareness to gender issues and women's human rights.
2. Review of curriculum and educational materials to include gender education and human rights issues
3. Removal of all references derogatory to the dignity of women from all public documents and legal instruments.
4. Use of different forms of mass media to communicate social messages relating to women's equality and empowerment.

The 73rd and 74th Amendments (1993) to the Indian Constitution have served as a breakthrough towards ensuring equal access and increased participation in political power structure for women. The PRIs will play a central role in the process of enhancing women's participation in public life. The PRIs and the local self Governments would be actively involved in the implementation and execution of the National Policy for Women at the grassroots level.

The involvement of voluntary organizations, associations, federations, trade unions, non-governmental organizations, women's organizations, as well as institutions dealing with education, training and research would be ensured in the formulation, implementation, monitoring and review of all policies and programmes affecting women. Towards this end, they would be provided with appropriate support related to resources and capacity building and facilitated to participate actively in the process of the empowerment of women.

The Policy will aim at implementation of international obligations/commitments in all sectors on empowerment of women such as the Convention on All Forms of Discrimination Against Women (CEDAW), Convention on the Rights of the Child (CRC), International Conference on Population and Development (ICPD+5) and other such instruments. International, regional and sub-regional cooperation towards the empowerment of women will continue to be encouraged through sharing of experiences, exchange of ideas and technology, networking with institutions and organizations and through bilateral and multi-lateral partnerships.

4

Problems of Women Entrepreneurs in India

4.1 Barriers Faced by Women Entrepreneurs

There are myriads of barriers facing entrepreneurs in India, including traditional cultural values that may favour acceptance of one's destiny and status as opposed to trying to improve one's material situation; social structures centring around the caste system; the history of British occupation, which has been critiqued as having forced out local businesses in favour of British business interests; and government practices since independence, which have tended toward state dominance of business, although this has been changing somewhat in recent years. Women entrepreneurs in India face all these barriers as well as additional obstacles directly and indirectly related to their gender.

Women's traditional roles in India have strongly constrained their activities at home, in the workplace and in the economy. They have also been disadvantaged in their access to resources, including food, transportation, education and literacy, technology, and financial resources in general, including financing for entrepreneurial activities.

The problems and constraints experienced by women entrepreneurs have resulted in restricting and inhibited the expansion of women entrepreneurship. The major barriers encountered by women entrepreneurs are:

4.1.1 Lack of Confidence: As women are accepting a subordinate status, as a result they lack confidence of their own capabilities. Even at home, family members do not have much faith in women possessing the abilities of decision-making.

4.1.2 Lack of Working Capital: To be women and to do

something in their own becomes quite difficult for them because of lack of access to funds as women do not possess any tangible security and credit in the market. Before marriage she has to depend on father and after marriage she has to follow the footsteps of the husband. As such, women do not enjoy the right over the property of any form and they have limited access over external sources of funds. Even getting loans from either a bank or financial institution becomes exceedingly difficult.

4.1.3 Socio-Cultural Barriers: Woman has to perform multiple roles, be it familial or social respective of her career as working woman or an entrepreneur. In our society, more importance is being given to male child as compared to female child. This mindset results in lack of schooling and necessary training for women.

Women are working in this multifaceted world. The organization scenario changes like a kaleidoscope with every responsibility, accountability and multiple pulls and pushes, which women have faced and come out with success.

In the new order, women will put down roots of a family and discover the freedom of sailing in the open seas. The women will visualize a new horizon and identify directions and make tough decisions. In the cacophony of sounds echoing of the past, the women will cross the threshold to listen to their own voices. The silence of centuries will find the first voice, which will beckon women to sail into the unknown and uncharted land to lay the foundations of their growth to contribute to a partnership.

4.2 Functions and Role of Women Entrepreneurs

According to Frederick Harbison, like a male entrepreneur, a women entrepreneur has five functions:

- Explore the prospects of starting new enterprises.
- Undertaking of risks and the handling of economic and non-economic uncertainties.
- Introduction of new innovations or imitation of successful

ones in existence.

- Co-ordination, administration and control.
- Supervision and providing leadership in all aspects of the business.

Risk taking and innovation are paramount for establishing or diversifying an enterprise. Co-ordination and supervision become increasingly important in improving the efficiency in the operation of the undertaking. Generally it is found that the same lady performs all these functions.

Modern writers have pointed out that women entrepreneurs are generally seen to undertake three types of industrial enterprises:

- Operate purely as a sub-contractor on raw materials provided by the customer.
- Manufacture items that are usually used by large scale units.
- Manufacture of consumer products which are directly sold in the market.

Women in business are a recent phenomenon in India. By and large they had confined themselves to petty business and tiny cottage industries. They engrossed themselves to professions like selling fruits and vegetables, and make pickles, papads and the like. Recent studies have revealed that several women are willing to become entrepreneurs due to various reasons. These reasons can be broadly classified into two: "Pull factors" and "Push Factors". Push factors imply the factors which encourage women to have an independent occupation. Under the influence of these factors the women entrepreneurs choose a profession as a challenge and as an adventure with an urge to do something new. Pull factors are those which compel women to take up business enterprises to get over financial difficulties and responsibility is thrust on them due to unfortunate family circumstances. However, the latter category forms only a negligible

The New Industrial Policy has stressed the importance of entrepreneurship among women. The NIP concedes that merely making larger resource allocation for women within the prevailing pattern and structure of development would not yield the desired results. The policy has a strategy for the holistic development of women. This would help develop their personality and at the same time improve their economic and social conditions. This policy, with this end in view, has redefined "women units" as units in which they had the majority shareholding and management control.

The Indian Women Entrepreneur thus has the ideal climate for exhibiting her talents. The Government does have the responsibility to improve the lot of women in economic life and prepare them to participate in industrial estates as entrepreneurs. On their own part, Indian woman have to overcome their own limitations. It is essential that Indian women must be ready to reach out for new jobs, new responsibilities and new experiences.

4.3 Problems of Women Entrepreneurs

The greatest difficulty to women entrepreneurs is the male chauvinism which is the order of the day. Therefore, women have a tendency to keep away from high flying economic activities which are supposedly regarded as the preserve of men. Even the financial institutions are sceptical of their entrepreneurial abilities to risk their funds on them. Seemingly non-partisan, even the bankers consider women loanees a higher risk than men loanees. They look for men behind the women applicants. They scare the women applicants with their greater and unwarranted inquisitiveness and put questions, sometimes embarrassing and some times incomprehensible often insisting on stiffer if not more unreasonable security considerations. The social setting is still not conducive as the men folk are less understanding and less co-operative, if not antagonistic to such enterprises by women.

The main problems faced by the women entrepreneurs can be stated as follows:

4.3.1 Financial Constraints: Like all small entrepreneurs, women entrepreneurs suffer from inadequate financial resources and working capital. They lack access to external funds due to their inability to provide tangible security. Very few women have property in their names. However, male members think it a big risk financing the ventures run by women. Banks have also taken a negative attitude while providing finance for women entrepreneurs. They discourage women borrowers on the belief that they can at any time leave their business and become housewives again. The result is women entrepreneurs are forced to rely on their own savings and loans from family or friends. The quantum of such funds is often negligible leading to failure of enterprises.

4.3.2 Over-dependence on Intermediaries: The enterprises run by women are characterised by inefficient arrangements for marketing and sale. The women entrepreneurs are most often dependent on intermediaries, who pocket a major part of the profits. It may be possible for the women to eliminate the middlemen, but then it will necessitate a lot of running about which may be difficult for the women entrepreneurs. Further, women entrepreneurs find it difficult to capture the market and make their products popular.

4.3.3 Scarcity of Raw Materials: Shortage of raw materials and other necessary inputs have sounded the death knell of many an enterprise run by women. On the one hand the prices of raw materials are very high and on the other they are able to get these raw materials at the minimum of discounts. A startling example is the failure of many women co-operatives in 1971 such as those engaged in basket making. This was mainly due to the inadequate availability of forest based raw materials.

4.3.4 Intense Competition: Women entrepreneurs face stiff competition for their products from organised industries and male entrepreneurs. Moreover, they do not have the organisational set up to pump in a lot of money for advertisement. They also have the mortification of being questioned about the quality of their product since it has been produced by women. This is despite the fact that women entrepreneurs are more sincere in maintaining the quality and time schedule.

4.3.5 High Cost of Production: Like most productive enterprises high cost of production has restricted the development of women enterprises. Some states like Kerala have programmes to assist women entrepreneurs by providing them with subsidies and tax concessions. But this is only in the initial stage of setting up an enterprise. When it comes to expansion of productive capacity and installation of new machinery, the help is negligible, dissuading many women entrepreneurs from venturing into new areas.

4.3.6 Low Mobility: Women entrepreneurs are greatly handicapped by their inability to travel from one place to another for business reasons. At the Governmental level, the licensing authorities, labour officers and sale s tax officials make life miserable for women by often asking all sorts of humiliating questions. Many are the cases where women have dropped out of business due to the difficulties caused to them by the officials forcing them to run from pillar to post.

4.3.7 Family Ties: In a country like India family ties are very strong. Here looking after the children and other members of the family are looked upon as the duty of a woman. Married women entrepreneurs have to make a fine balance between business and home. Their success greatly depends on the support given by the family. One can see in India that behind the success of a female entrepreneur there is always the unstinted support of the family or the woman concerned is a spinster without any family responsibilities. Occupational backgrounds of families and education level of husbands have a direct bearing on the development of women entrepreneurship.

4.3.8 Social Attitudes: This is regarded as the most important stumbling block in the path of women entrepreneurship. Despite constitutional equality, there is widespread discrimination against women. In a male dominated society women do not get equal treatment. This is specially so in the rural areas of India. Rural women have the potential, but they lack adequate training. There is common belief that skill imparted to a girl is lost when she gets married. Therefore, girls continue to be helpers in agriculture and handicrafts and the rigid social attitudes prevent them from becoming successful and independent entrepreneurs.

4.3.9 Adverse Effects of Risk Bearing: Women in this country have led a protected life. This has reduced their ability to bear economic and other risks of business. Moreover, the impacts of losses are more severe on women since they lack sufficient social support. They live in a society where people wait to chastise the enterprising and the intensity will be greater in the case of women. Besides many women entrepreneurs lack the necessary initiative, suffer from inferiority complex and are easily disheartened by failure.

4.3.10 Lack of Education: Due to the lack of education, many women are unaware of the latest technological developments and market trends. This creates further problems in the setting up and running of business enterprises. Studies have revealed that uneducated women do not have their own system of accounting which may be sufficient to run a petty business, but certainly not a business enterprise.

4.3.11 Low Need for Achievement: The most important pre-requisites for success in entrepreneurship are need for achievement, independence and autonomy. But in India the common Indian women is happy to bask in the glory of her parents, husbands, children etc. They have preconceived notions about their role in life and this inhibits achievement and independence. In the absence of the required urge to achieve, few women succeed as entrepreneurs.

In fact development of women entrepreneurship can be an integral part of all development efforts. It is indeed a step in the right direction that a special chapter covered the integration of women in economic development. In this regard the plan document suggested the following:

- To treat women as specific target groups in all development programmes.
- To properly diversify vocational training facilities for women to suit their varied needs and skills.
- To encourage appropriate technologies, equipment and practice for reducing their drudgery and increasing their efficiency and productivity.
- To provide marketing assistance at the State Level.
- To increase women's participation in decision making.

5

Efforts to Increase Women Entrepreneurship in India

5.1 Role of Government

The Indian government has been involved in efforts to increase local entrepreneurship since the 1950s including a government program of reservations and a subsidy system for university graduates. These efforts have been criticised as both ineffective and more concerned with patronage networks and bribery than with a strong small business sector. The government has also been criticized for the many regulatory bottlenecks and for its failure to make sufficient progress on infrastructure improvements. The Ministry of Industry established the National Institute for Entrepreneurship and Small Business Development, which has focused on entrepreneurship development through training programs, and has produced educational manuals and videos. It is not clear if most or even many of the Indian government's effort in the area of entrepreneurship have adequately addressed the particular needs of women.

5.2 Role of Multinational Corporations (MNCs)

A variety of institutions have addressed the need to increase entrepreneurship in India. For many years, the lack of success of many multinational companies in countries such as India has been related to MNC's insensitivity to host countries, including a failure to adapt products to local needs lack of recognition of negative effects of their products on local social and economic conditions, and notably, a failure to find ways for local businesses to participate. Some MNC's today follow variety of practices to address these concerns, including adapting product and marketing strategies to local situations, hiring local employees whenever possible and using local enterprises as suppliers and distributors. However, the latter of these practices has often been limited in application. To the extent that India's economy since independence has been closed, there has been close involvement of MNC's than could have been the case. Some observers welcome the recent increase in the openness of the Indian Economy and would like to see it become more so, while others are more critical of the role MNC's are playing in India. With respect to gender, there has been little attention paid by MNC's to the empowerment of women entrepreneurs, but MNC critics have noted that many of the small scale enterprises disrupted by MNC activities either often employ women or are run by women.

5.3 Role of Non-governmental Organisations (NGOs)

Perhaps the most effective type of organization in the efforts to foster entrepreneurship in India in general, and among women especially, has been the NGO. A number of NGOs have initiated programs related to entrepreneurship, including micro credit or microfinance programs for small scale entrepreneurs; training and technology transfer projects; and direct assistance with small business start ups. With due respect to women, NGOs sometimes offer programs targeted specifically at women, since women may have limited or no access to more generalized development programs.

NGO's operating the developing countries such as India, whether based in India or abroad, often focus on small entrepreneurs and/or the special development needs of women by providing training, workshops, technical assistance, job opportunities and help with start up of small businesses. Often, NGOs receive funding or other assistance from government, charitable or corporate organizations. In India, these efforts have ranged from the Indian Government's National Institute for Entrepreneurship and Small Business Development to the non-profit, locally based Self Employed Women's Association (SEWA) and Hindustan Lever Ltd.'s corporate based program to encourage distribution of its product through local entrepreneurs.

5.4 Micro Credit Programme

Micro credit programs in the economic development context refer to the extension of banking financial services to the poor, who otherwise would be unlikely to have access to services such as small loans and taking deposits. When traditional banks are involved, micro credit is typically provided in a conventional manner. When governments have subsidized credit programs with the goal of reaching the poor, there is evidence that such programs have been subverted, with the wealthy in the society reaping the benefits from the subsidies.[16] There are also some examples of foreign companies using micro credit programs for local entrepreneurs to gain access to rural markets by extending credit to small distributors of their products, which are sometimes either sold in smaller units or in simpler forms in order to increase their usefulness to poor, rural customers. When NGOs are involved, the poor may participate in a revolving loan fund, where the NGO may put up the initial seed money for the loan fund, and the clients repay loans that are then re-loaned to other small entrepreneurs so that the community is essentially acting as its own bank. This has been referred to as "village banking".[18] Recently, the 2006 Nobel Peace Prize was awarded to Bangladeshi economist and banker Muhammad Yunus for his work with micro-credit in Bangladesh and he brought nine women borrowers with him to Norway to accept the prize.

5.5 Entrepreneurship Development Programme (EDP)

With this background, the Government and financial organisations started thinking in terms of fostering entrepreneurship through training interventions. Towards this, a pioneering initiative was jointly taken by Gujarat Industrial Investment Corporation (GIIC) and other state agencies in Gujarat, in the late sixties. A 3-month training programme known as EDP was evolved. The Programme was meant for new and selected entrepreneurs who had latent entrepreneurial potential. It laid emphasis on

- Setting up a small venture.
- Managing it.
- Making profits out of it.

The initial programmes were oriented towards business knowledge and skills. Later, behavioural inputs (Especially, Achievement Motivation Training – AMT) were also made regular features of the training package.

Entrepreneurship Development Programmes (EDPs) which began as an experiment by Gujarat State Industrial Corporation, gained momentum at the national level in the early seventies. At the same time, SIET initiated EDPs in the state of Jammu and Kashmir; and Small Industries Development Organisation (SIDO) started conducting EDPs for unemployed engineers through its Small Industries Service Institutes (SISIs) Industrial Development Bank of India (IDBI) also evinced interest in the approach and circulated a paper on the achievements and potential of the Gujarat experience among various state Governments. Subsequently IDBI encouraged Technical Consultancy Organisations (TCOs)—a creation of the All India Financial Institutions—to launch EDPs in their respective states, by providing funding support encouraging results as well as need to spread the programme to all the districts of Gujarat, led to creation of the Centre for Entrepreneurship Development (CED) in Ahmedabad in 1979. It was the first specialised institute of its kind in the country, exclusively devoted to the task of Entrepreneurship Development.

Encouraged and impressed by the success of CED, All India Financial Institutions, viz. Industrial Development Bank of India (IDBI), Industrial Financial Corporation of India (IFCI), Industrial Credit and Investment Corporation of India (ICICI) and State Bank of India (SBI) with active support of the Government of Gujarat, sponsored a national resource organisation, viz. Entrepreneurship Development Institute of India (EDI-I) in 1983. It was entrusted with the task of spreading institutionalizing ED activities in the country. Government of India later also set-up the National Institute of Entrepreneurship and Small Business Development (NIESBUD) to coordinate ED efforts at the national level. Subsequently, some of the state Governments, with the support of All India Financial Institutions, also took initiative in establishing state level Institutes of Entrepreneurship Development (IEDs) like IED Lucknow (UP), IED Bhubaneshwar (Orissa), IED Patna (Bihar); or state centres such as Maharashtra Centre for Entrepreneurship Development, Aurangabad (Maharashtra), Madhya Pradesh Centre for Entrepreneurship Development of Karnataka, Dharwad (Karnataka) in order to take the ED activities down to grass-roots level.

At present a large number of institutions and organisations are engaged in conducting a variety of training and research activities directed towards developing entrepreneurship. According to a study conducted by NIESBUD, about 686 organisations (which include District Industries Centres, or DICs) are engaged in conducting Entrepreneurship Development Programmes in the country. Most of these organisations are established, sponsored and/or financially supported (directly or indirectly) by the central/state Governments, financial institutions and public sector banks.

All India Financial Institutions, viz., IDBI, IFCI, ICICI, besides SBI and the Governments at the centre (through its Department of Science and Technology) as well as the state level, and some commercial banks have been funding, supporting and organising Entrepreneurship Development Programmes especially since 1978 in a big way.

The need of the present day is, therefore, to promote development in such a way that the first and foremost priority shall be given to women's skill development and education to alter current inequality. Women have plunged into the field of small enterprises as entrepreneurs. During the last two decades, India has been successful to a great degree in fostering the growth of small enterprises.

5.6 Women Entrepreneurship Development (WED) Programme

The main objective of the WED programme is Human Resources Development with a view to strengthening and accelerating the growth of women's micro and small enterprises. As such, the trainer needs to understand the three main stages of pre-training, training and post training of the entire women entrepreneurship development process.

5.6.1 Pre-training Stage: At this stage, a trainer has to:

- Conduct the training needs assessment to determine the regional potential of the training centre (village or a cluster of villages, small town, city);
- Create awareness about the programme among women;
- Establish liaison with local support organisations; and
- Identify and select potential women for the training programme.

The trainer also needs to study the socio-economic environment of the centre and identify viable business opportunities consistent with the skills and knowledge of the potential women entrepreneurs.

5.6.2 Training Stage: Based on the successful experience of training and developing women entrepreneurs, a training programme has been designed to lead women towards enterprise development activities over a four week period (intact or as separate modules). The training inputs are designed to develop capabilities required to start and run an enterprise successfully.

5.6.3 Post-training Stage:

- In the post-training period, the trainer has to help and guide participants to implement their business plans, assist them in completing formalities as well as procure finance for setting up the enterprise. The support should continue until the women establish their units and manage them successfully, especially in developing market linkages.

- Follow-up, monitoring and evaluation.

It is, therefore, significant to know the existing levels of knowledge, skills and competencies of potential women entrepreneurs, identify the gap between 'existing' and 'desired' levels, and design a training programme to prepare women for enterprise creation and management. The trainer should understand the "gaps" in skills, knowledge and attitudes of the women intending to undertake entrepreneurial activities.

The identified and selected group of women for a specific WED programme should be as homogeneous as possible. Differences in education and social and economic background can hamper the group dynamics and make it difficult to meet the needs of individual participants.

The trainer will also need to be aware of the demands which the new enterprise will make on the women initiating, establishing and running their business. Details of training needs can be identified by comparing the present status of the women with the skills, knowledge and attitudes required in enterprise creation and management. Hence, the following data should be systematically collected to find out the training needs of the potential women entrepreneurs.

- Personal and family background in terms of occupation, income level etc.
- Educational background, either through formal or informal education;
- Work experience and exposure to outside world, particularly the work environment;
- Knowledge and skills relevant to entrepreneurship;
- Readiness to spare time for training and business creation, considering other social and family roles and responsibilities;
- Analysis of anticipated entrepreneurial functions as compared to present status and activities;

- Details of current knowledge, skills, and behaviour and the needs to upgrade these for satisfactorily running an enterprise.

The trainer should assess the support needs which women require for establishing enterprises, and try to mobilize such support by developing a strategy for institutional networking. The support needs assessment may be undertaken by assessing.

- Women's perception regarding the level of support needs and facilities available;
- The level of actual support available, in terms of what is offered by existing institutions;
- The need to sensitize the existing enterprise support system to provide a conducive and gender sensitive environment for women Entrepreneurship Development.

The success of WED programmes very much depends on the availability of support from both government as well as non-government institutions. Therefore, the trainer will need to assess the possibility of actively involving support institutions in WED programmes and identify possible linkage for assistance with finance, markets and infrastructure. The assessment should collect details of:

- Government policies and priorities for small and micro enterprise development in general, and for women in particular;
- Schemes and incentives offered by various support institutions to women entrepreneurs;
- Credit support available and possible linkages for the same;
- Infrastructure availability in terms of land, buildings (working sheds, etc.), basic utilities like water, power, transport, communication, etc.
- Gender sensitivity of agencies towards supporting women entrepreneurs; possibility of institutional linkages for marketing;
- Support and resource needs for conducting WED training,

such as availability of training faculty, advisers, classroom facility, etc.

It is necessary that the trainers study and assess the environment within which the women intend to establish their enterprises. A woman's role may involve a lot of social responsibilities, and even today, there may be some places where women are not very well accepted as fully fledged entrepreneurs. The developmental needs assessment study should aim to:

- Identify problems encountered in promotion of small and micro enterprises in general, and for women entrepreneur in particular.
- Study the existing developmental scenario and environment impacting on women taking up entrepreneurship in the area where the WED programme is proposed.

While assessing developmental needs, the following factors should be studied by the trainer. WED can be initiated if these are found favourable or if the trainers identify opportunities to make them more conducive through planned initiatives.

- Community/family's attitude towards women and the development of women's enterprises;
- Local development plans and stated commitments to women development;
- The impact and results of earlier developmental work in general, and of women development in particular.

5.6.4 Awareness Building and Networking: The trainer will have to work out a suitable promotional process to create awareness amongst potential women entrepreneurs in the different target groups. Not every woman aspires to become an entrepreneur and so promotional activities should be directed towards those who are most interested and who are likely to pursue a career in entrepreneurship. In addition, there may not be sufficient financial resources to train and develop all those who desire to become entrepreneurs. Therefore, resources should be aimed at those women who are most likely to succeed in enterprise. The promotional activities can be targeted at those who are "serious" about business. The selection procedures should identify those with the greatest interest, commitment and potential.

5.6.5 Sensitization Workshops and Networking: Sensitization of relevant agencies and networking for WED should involve arranging meetings, discussions, exhibitions and workshops or seminars. This should be directed at two segments:

- Supporting agencies such as banks, industry departments, women support agencies, NGOs, and the other key factors in the WED support system;
- Women entrepreneurs from different groups and social strata.

The WED trainer should undertake these activities in accordance with the finding of the earlier needs assessment study. During sensitization, it is important to clearly describe the potential role of women entrepreneurs in development issues. In order to build up the required network for organisational support, staff from the promotional and support agencies need to be appraised of the processes involved in developing women entrepreneurs, the likely expectations of women, relevant gender issues, the barriers and constraints faced by women entrepreneurs, and the opportunities and potential for the development of women entrepreneurs. This will help to create a better understanding about WED and will subsequently encourage the agencies to support and assist women entrepreneurs.

5.6.6 Identification and Selection of Potential Women Entrepreneurs: It has been demonstrated that the path to an entrepreneurial career passes through considerably complex ups and downs. Training alone cannot be expected to instil completely new aptitudes and capabilities in individual women. Therefore, the identification and selection of women with latent entrepreneurial competencies becomes very important.

The socialization process of women in many countries does not encourage them to develop appropriate entrepreneurial attitudes and behavioural competencies, such as goal-setting, initiative taking, problem-solving, etc. With so many agencies (both government and non-government) now involved in promoting the development of women, an important shift from "welfare" orientation to "Development" orientation has been experienced.

There are also many practical considerations involved in achieving success in the development of small and micro businesses/enterprises through the WED programmes. Developing the credibility and acceptability of the WED programmes is also very important. A strong commitment to this strategy among support institutions, particularly banks and government agencies, needs to be developed. Hence it is important to develop a scientific and well validated approach in selecting the targeted groups of potential women entrepreneurs.

There is an important sequence in developing the abilities and capabilities for becoming entrepreneurs. These are generally called the appropriate entrepreneurial competencies required for effective performance in an enterprise. These are:

- Knowledge for enterprise building;
- Managerial skills;
- Entrepreneurial attitude and behavioural skills and competencies;
- Motives and Motivations.

Identification and selection can involve a lot of time and money. Initially, it may lead to a reduction in the number of entrepreneurs registered on a WED programme. But it will soon be realised that the time and money spent on selection procedures is a real investment. It will enable trainers to select the most competent women who display entrepreneurial capabilities. Identifying and selecting entrepreneurs is a combination of psycho-cultural and economic exercises, which requires a certain amount of training and orientation. The trainers involved in this task should be familiar with the concepts and methods before trying them out in the field. Selection procedures aim to:

- Assess the potential of women who are eager to become entrepreneurs to find out if they have potential entrepreneurial competencies;
- Select those who, by virtue of their behavioural and entrepreneurial profiles, have a better probability of success.

5.6.7 Selection of Tools and Techniques: Research shows that entrepreneurs possess certain attitudinal and behavioural competencies which distinguish them from others. These Personal Entrepreneurial Competencies (PECs) are the behavioural indications of achievement oriented entrepreneurs. The specially designed selection tools given here have been validated in many countries, and they help in assessing the motives, knowledge, and behavioural skills related to entrepreneurship. The selection procedure can be implemented in two stages:

Stage 1: Bio-data questionnaire

Stage 2: Overall assessment interview

5.6.8 Curriculum Development: Trainers need to know how to design a need-based training programme. The objective of any WED training is to develop potential women entrepreneurs, and enable and equip them to establish and manage their own enterprises successfully. If they are already in business, training in selected inputs should strengthen and improve their performance.

The trainers should aim to familiarise women participants with conceptual knowledge, as well as getting practical information and skills relevant to day to day business operations. The desired outcome of WED training is to see women initiate and develop in their own economic activities in a sustainable manner. The curriculum should be developed in such a way that it can meet the needs of different target groups in different areas. The WED curriculum should be developed in such a way that it can meet the needs of different target groups in different areas. The WED curriculum should be a completely integrated package to develop the knowledge, skills and competencies related to managing an enterprise. It should cover the following aspects.

- Knowledge and information inputs regarding entrepreneurial actions and decisions;
- Entrepreneurial attitudes and behaviour development;
- Managerial skills development.

The following functions are essential to successfully establishing and managing an enterprise.

Although these functions are necessary for any level of operation of enterprise, the trainer must examine them and assess their suitability from three different angles:

- The entrepreneur herself and her development;
- Enterprise building and establishment;
- Enterprise management for survival and growth.

5.6.9 Detailed Curriculum for WED

A. Initiating an Enterprise: For a woman to initiate an enterprise she should have a good knowledge of the following:

1. Identification and selection of product;
2. Preparation of project plan;
3. Consolidation of Resources.

Identification and Selection of Product:

- Project Identification and generating ideas;
- Criteria for assessing and selecting new business;
- Identifying business opportunities;
- Competency-building, Seeking opportunities;
- Feasibility of small enterprise;
- Sources of information and guidance for new business opportunities;
- Selection of technology;
- How to add new products to existing ones.

Preparation of Project Plan

- Assessing feasibility of a product : technical, financial, marketing and commercial;

- Assessing market potential;
- Determining the size of unit and investment;
- Working capital estimation;
- Choosing appropriate technology, infrastructure and staff requirements;
- Financial calculations, funds and cash flow;
- Calculating cost of production and profitability.

Consolidation of Resources

- Awareness building and understanding the peculiarities and problem of women entrepreneurs;
- Finding the sources of information "Whom to contact for what"
- Knowing the prevailing government policies and incentives essential for enterprise creation;
- Understanding the procedural requirement for setting up business/industry.

B. Enterprise Establishment and Management: At the initial stages as a single proprietor, the woman entrepreneur alone fulfils several functions in her enterprise. These functions are mainly in the areas of Marketing, Production, Finance and Human Resource Management.

C. Entrepreneurial Behavioural Skills & Competency Development:

- Potential women entrepreneurs require the motivation necessary to sustain their efforts and commitment while implementing their plans and operating their enterprise. One of the main characteristics of an entrepreneur is the need to achieve; this enables the entrepreneurs to set realistic goals on the basis of self analysis, as well as an awareness of one's strengths and weaknesses.
- Persuasion and Influencing Strategies: She uses a variety of strategies to influence or persuade others so as to accomplish her set objectives;
- Goal Setting: She articulates long range vision and goals. She continuously sets, monitors and revises short range

objectives.

- Risk Taking: She takes personal responsibility, welcomes challenges and takes calculated and moderate risks.

D. Evaluation: The objectives of the WED Programme are not simply to impart theoretical training but to contribute to tangible results in seeing women establish micro and small enterprises. Therefore, in order to improve the effectiveness of WED programmes, the trainer needs to give support and guidance once the training is over. Therefore, timely co-ordination, access to adequate finance, and availability of requisite infrastructure should be facilitated through a well-planned follow-up strategy as this can be a critical pre-condition for the success of WED programmes.

Even with the most careful and systematic planning, a WED programme curriculum may not be perfect. In the design process it is impossible to identify and analyse all the positive factors which should be taken into consideration while implementing WED training in a particular situation and with a specific target group. There can be no guarantee that the expected outcome of enterprise creation will be realized however, adequate provision should be made to provide support and establish networking arrangements right from the stage of curriculum design. Schemes available with banks for working capital finance are: (a) cash credit scheme, which is a funding arrangement of a major percentage on the value of work in process, finished goods and receivables and (b) other working capital finance schemes are venture capital funding, factoring, discounting letter of credit facility etc.

Schemes available for financing fixed assets and machinery are: (a) term loan, (b) lease finance, (c) hire purchase finance, (d) suppliers bill discounting scheme and (e) deferred payment credit scheme

6

Programmes and Schemes for Women Entrepreneurs

The integrated schemes of assistance to women entrepreneurs which provide for identification, selection, training and consultancy and escort services apart from term loan facilities and terms continue to receive increasing response. As a result, assistance to women entrepreneurs is increasing day by day. Some of the schemes introduced to provide financial assistance entrepreneurs are briefly summarized.

6.1 Small Industry Development Bank of India's (SIDBI) Scheme of Assistance for Women Entrepreneurs

SIDBI has special schemes for assistance to women entrepreneurs. These are aimed at providing training and extension service support to women entrepreneurs according to their skills and social financial assistance on concessional terms to enable them to set up small enterprises.

The schemes are operated through State Financial Corporation (SFCs), State Industrial Corporations (SIDCs), Commercial Banks, State Cooperative Banks and Regional Rural Refinance Institutions. For instance A.P State Financial Corporation (APSFC) provides assistance in the form of term loans for women entrepreneurs is expected to contribute at least 15 percent of the project cost. The entrepreneur has to repay the loan over eight years, in moratorium period of two years.

6.2 Bank of India's Priyadarshini Yojana

Under this scheme the bank provides long term and working capital assistance under the categories:

- Professional and self-employed, e.g. chartered accountants, lawyers and doctors.
- Small Business, e.g. beauty parlour, laundry and circulating library.
- Retail traders, e.g. fair price shops, general provision stores.
- Village or Cottage and Small Scale Industry Road Transport Operators Allied agricultural activity.

The maximum loan amount sanctioned depends on the entrepreneur needs with limits for term loans and up to Rs. 1 lakh for working capital. Interest rates depend upon the range from 12 percent (for loans up to Rs. 2 lakh). The contribution margin will be about 20 percent, depending upon the type of activity intended to:

In addition, women entrepreneurs are also eligible for finance under the following government sponsored programme.

- Prime Minister's Rozgar Yojana (PMRY)
- Self Employment Programme for Urban Poor (SEPUP)
- Integrated Rural Development Programme (IRDP)

6.2.1 Scheme of Interest Subsidy for Women Entrepreneurs: The main objective of the scheme of interest subsidy for Women Entrepreneurs is to the women with business acumen and entrepreneurial traits.

All industrial projects whether in rural, cottage, tiny, small and medium scale (i.e. with Rs. 3 crore) sectors, if set up by women entrepreneur(s) will be covered under the scheme shall be operated through the State Financial Corporations (SFCs)/State level institutions granting assistance to women entrepreneurs for setting up their industrial rural, cottage, tiny, small and medium scale sector.

To be eligible for availing herself of the subsidy under the scheme, a woman entrepreneur with the following criteria is selected:

- The woman entrepreneur should be unemployed before taking up the venture. The venture should be her first venture. The woman entrepreneur must have been sanctioned and disbursed finance by SFC or a State level financial institution.

- The assistance under the scheme takes the form of one time subsidy and is equivalent interest payable by the industrial unit set up by the woman entrepreneur to the SFC for the loan assistance sanctioned for the project for a period to a ceiling of Rs. 25,000 per annum.

In addition to the above there are several schemes offered by various state government agencies.

6.3 Industrial Development Bank of India's (IDBI) Mahila Udyam Nidhi (MUN) Scheme

IDBI has set up a special fund, Mahila Udyam Nidhi with a Corpus of Rs. 5 crore to provide assistance to women entrepreneurs, intending to set up projects in SSI sector. This being implemented by SIDBI.

Women Entrepreneurs owning and managing an enterprise with a minimum financial equity are eligible for assistance provided the project cost excluding, working capital does not exceed Rs. 10 lakh. The debt equity ratio should be 3:1. The assistance will be provided in the form of soft loan up to a maximum of 15 percent of fixed capital in equity. Minimum promoter's contribution insisted upon is 10 percent of the fixed cost.

A nominal service charge of 1 percent per annum is charged, which is payable annually. They should be repaid over a period not exceeding 10 years including as initial moratorium years. In this scheme, seed capital assistance is provided without insisting on security.

6.4 Mahila Vikas Nidhi (MVN) Scheme

Recognizing the role of voluntary agencies in improving the socio economic status to set up a special development fund, Mahila Vikas Nidhi, with an initial allocation from its technical assistance fund. Assistance by way of grant and soft loan would be from the Nidhi to such voluntary organizations working exclusively for women and the organization with a properly constituted governing body. Agencies with a proven record in managing income generating programmes would be eligible to receive aid under the scheme such as setting up of training cum development centres, skill up gradation, skill up gradation programmes, programmes or marketing as management up gradation and such other industrial activities which improve the women would be eligible for support under the MVN. The Assistance under the scheme towards one time capital expenditure, the recurring expenses being met by the voluntary funds or grants/donations from government or other agencies.

6.5 State Bank of India's (SBI) Stree Shakti Package

The SBI introduced a new package of November, 1989 aimed at reinforcing its efforts it developing entrepreneurship among women. Concessional and facilities are here under.

An important highlight of the package is conducting of Entrepreneurial Development Programme (EDP) exclusively designed for women all over the country with the help of Training College and local branches.

The branch managers along with field staff would provide the necessary in assistance to those women who do not plan to set up full fledged industrial ventures do something at home. In this scheme for Loans of up to Rs. 25000 neither the guarantee margin money is taken from borrowers. Further a discount of half a percent is allowed charged. The loan proposals received from women entrepreneurs would be sanctioned within 20 days except in cases of proposals for high value and also where other financials are involved.

According to the Third All India Census of Small Scale Industries conducted in 2001-02 subsequent estimates made, only 10.11 percent of the Micro and Small Enterprises in India are owned by women while 9.46 percent of the MSE enterprises are managed by women. As per latest available estimates, the number of women owned and women managed enterprise are 12.99 lakh and 12.15 lakh respectively.

In order to encourage more and more women enterprises in the MSE sector, several new schemes have been formulated by the Ministry and some more are in the process of being fir targeted only at the development of women enterprises in India.

6.6 Eleventh Five Year Plan (2007-12) on Women Empowerment

India has committed to meeting the Millennium Development Goals and is a signatory to many international conventions, including Convention for Elimination of all forms of Discrimination against Women and the Convention on the Rights of the Child. Yet, at the start of the Eleventh Five Year Plan, women and children continue to be victims of violence, neglect and injustice. The Eleventh Plan will address these problems by looking at gender as a cross-cutting theme. It will recognize women's agency and the need for women's empowerment. At the same time it will ensure the survival, protection and all round development of children of all ages, communities and economic groups.

Women are significant contributors to the growing economy and children are assets of the future. Almost fifty per cent of our population today comprises of women while 42 percent is under the age of 18. For growth to be truly inclusive, we have to ensure their protection, well-being, development, empowerment and participation.

The vision of the Eleventh Five Year Plan is to end the multifaceted exclusions and discriminations faced by women and children; to ensure that every woman and child in the country is able to develop to her/his full potential and share the benefits of economic growth and prosperity. Success will depend on our ability to adopt a participatory approach that empowers women and children and makes them partners in their own development. The roadmap for this has already been laid in the National Policy on Women 2001 and the National Plan of Action for Children 2005.

The Eleventh Plan recognizes that women and children are not homogenous categories; they belong to diverse castes, classes, communities, economic groups, and are located within a range of geographic and development zones. Consequently, some groups are more vulnerable than others. Mapping and addressing the specific deprivations that arise from these multiple locations is essential for the success of planned interventions. Thus apart from the general programme interventions, special targeted interventions, catering to the differential needs of these groups will be undertaken during the Eleventh Plan.

In the Eleventh Plan, for the first time, women are recognised not just as equal citizens but as agents of economic and social growth. The approach to gender equity is based on the recognition that interventions in favour of women must be multi-pronged and they must (i) provide women with basic entitlements (ii) address the reality of globalization and its impact on women by prioritizing economic empowerment (iii) ensure an environment free from all forms of violence against women– physical, economic, social, psychological, and (iv) ensure the participation and adequate representation of women at the highest policy levels, particularly in Parliament and Assemblies (v) strengthen existing institutional mechanisms and create new ones for gender mainstreaming and effective policy implementation.

6.6.1 Status of Women: Due to the untiring efforts of the women's movement, the country amended and enacted women-related legislations during the Tenth Plan. The Married Women's Property Act (1874), the Hindu Succession Act (1956) were amended and the Protection of Women from Domestic Violence Act, (2005) was passed. The Union Budget 2005-06, for the first time, included a separate statement highlighting the gender sensitivities of the budgetary allocation under 10 demands for grants. Gender Budgeting Cells were set up in 52 Central Ministries/Departments to review public expenditure, collect gender disaggregated data and conduct gender based impact analysis.

6.6.2 Work and Employment: Entrenched patriarchal norms and customs mean that women's work goes unnoticed and is unpaid for. The double burden of work placed on her (unrecognized household work and low pay in recognized work) coupled with social norms that prevent her from getting the requisite educational and technical skills result in a low female work participation rate, either real or statistical. Female workforce participation rate in India was 28 percent (2004) as compared to other developing nations like Sri Lanka (30 percent), Bangladesh (37 percent) and South Africa (38 percent).

A sectoral breakdown of women workers reveals that 32.9 percent are cultivators, 38.9 percent agricultural labourers (as against 20.9 percent men) and 6.5 percent workers in the household industry. Much of the increase in employment among women has been in the form of self-employment; 48 per cent of urban and 64 percent of rural women workers describe themselves as "self-employed". The Tenth Plan has, however, seen a welcome increase in the share of regular employment among female workers in urban India.

As in the case of education, women's employment characterisation differs across communities. The Sachar Committee Report shows that work participation rate among Muslim women is 25 percent, and as low as 18 percent in urban areas. A larger proportion (73 percent) of Muslim women is self-employed compared to 55 percent Hindu women. A much smaller proportion of SC/ST women are self-employed; 45 percent of SC/ST women are casual workers compared to around 20 percent Muslim and 15 percent of upper caste Hindu women.

Another worrying fact is that despite a slight increase in employment, the average earning for rural women has declined between 1999-2000 and 2004-05. This decline is more pronounced among poorer women i.e. illiterate women and women who have dropped out of primary, secondary or higher secondary. The average wage for men has, on the other hand, shown an increase across all categories, leading to a widening of the wage disparity ratio (ratio of female wage/male wage) from 0.89 in 1999-00 to 0.59 in 2004-05 for rural and 0.83 in 1999-00 and 0.75 in 2004-05 in urban areas, for all categories.

6.6.3 Unorganized Sector: On an average, unorganized sector workers earn one-fourth the wage of organized sector workers, often doing similar jobs. It is estimated that 118 million workers or 97 percent of the female work force are involved in the unorganized sector. Agriculture is the main employer of women informal workers. 75 percent of the total female work force and 85 percent of rural women are employed in agriculture as wage workers or workers on own/contracted household farms. As men migrate to non-farm jobs; there has been an increasing feminization of agriculture. But even as the face of the farmer becomes increasingly female, few women have direct access to agricultural land affecting their ability to optimize agricultural productivity.

The non-agriculture segment of the informal sector engages 27 million workers or 23 percent of the female work force. It estimated that more than half the 31 million construction workers in India (90 percent of them informal) are women. The seasonality of work and the lack of alternate avenues lead to exploitation and ensure that these women remain the poorest and most vulnerable.

6.6.4 Home-based Workers: Due to lack of qualifications and training, absence of childcare support, loss of formal employment, social and cultural constraints and absence of alternatives, around 57 percent of working women are home-based workers. As home based work is sometimes the only alternative for the poorest communities, it inevitably involves children, especially girls.

6.6.5 Services Sector: The number of women in the services sector has increased. According to NSSO data, in

2000, 12 percent of the female work force was employed in the tertiary sector. Women, however, remain underrepresented in higher level and higher paid jobs. The biggest single increase after apparels, has been among those employed in private households. More than 3 million women or over 12 per cent of all women workers in urban India work as domestic servants. These women are poorly paid and often are forced to work under harsh conditions. It is also important to note that nearly 60 percent of the women from the organized sector are employed in community, social and personnel services.

6.6.6 Women in the Unorganized Sector: The Eleventh Plan recognizes that women in the unorganized sector need social security covering issues of leave, wages, work conditions, pension, housing, child care, health benefits, maternity benefits, safety and occupational health, and complaints committee for sexual harassment. While it is difficult to tackle some of these issues immediately due to the nature of unorganized enterprises, steps will be taken to ensure safety, childcare facilities, toilets etc for women. The Plan will ensure increased availability of micro-credit to women in the unorganized sector.

6.6.7 Women in Agriculture: The challenge in the Eleventh Plan is to improve the availability of agricultural inputs, credit, marketing facilities, technology and skill training for the increasing number of women farmers. Resource pooling and group investment, financial and infrastructural support will be provided. Women in Agriculture will be on the top of the Eleventh Plan agenda and a two-pronged strategy will be adopted: (a) Ensuring effective and independent land rights for women and (b) Strengthening women's agricultural capacities.

A specific scheme will be devised by M/o WCD for identifying and helping women in states where agrarian crisis has ravaged families. Women's vulnerabilities resulting from farmer suicides due to crop failure and inability to pay loans will be addressed.

6.6.8 Land Rights for Women: Land rights not only empower women economically but strengthen their ability to challenge social and political inequities. The Eleventh Plan will carry out a range of initiatives to enhance women's land access. It will ensure direct transfers to them through land reforms, anti-poverty programmes and resettlement schemes. It will include individual or group titles to women in all government land transfers, credit support to poor women to purchase or lease land, records and legal support for women's inheritance rights, incentives and subsidies on women owned land. The group approach to women's ownership of land and productive assets will be explored and appropriate linkages will be made with the SHG movement. In case of displacement, a gender sensitive rehabilitation policy that includes equitable allocation of land to women will be devised. The Eleventh Plan will also ensure the rights of poor, landless and tribal women over forest land, commons and other resources.

6.6.9 Impact of Globalisation and Eleventh Plan Strategy: Liberalization has led to a paradigm shift in the country's economy. We have moved towards technology dominated sectors. While this has provided increased opportunities, it has also posed challenges. Many traditional livelihoods which have high employment potential like handlooms and other home based non-agro enterprises which are women dominated, have become unviable. Wage differentials, job vulnerability and unpaid work burden for women has increased, while their social safety nets have been eroded. Unequal access for women to schooling, land, credit facilities, alternate employment, skill training and technology has led to the crowding of women in the lowly paid jobs of most sectors. The Eleventh Plan will examine the impact of globalization on women, especially poor women including gender differentials in wage rates, exploitation of women in the unorganized sector, lack of skill training, technology and marketing support etc. While seeking to provide relief to deprived and women dominated sectors i.e. agriculture, small enterprises, the Plan will also work towards mainstreaming women in new and emerging areas of the economy through necessary skill training, vocational training and technology education. It will work towards a social security policy that mitigates the negative impact of globalization on women.

6.6.10 Women in the Services Sector: The challenge in the Eleventh Plan is to promote women's participation, especially in areas where there is a poor gender ratio. This will entail special tax incentives for women headed enterprises, women employees, firms employing more women and women entrepreneurial ventures. The Plan will encourage private public partnerships and corporate social responsibility programs for women's training, capacity building and empowerment.

In view of the large number of women employed as domestic workers, the plan will make attempts to organize them and frame regulations with respect to hours of work, holidays etc for them. Cases of brutality and abuse will be registered immediately and legal support will be provided to the domestic workers to prevent their exploitation.

6.6.11 Skill Development: Globalization has put a premium on skills and higher levels of education, which are often out of reach of women in the unorganized sector. A key issue in the Eleventh Plan is to enable these women to secure higher level and better paid jobs through vocational training and skill development. Women need technology support, credit facilities and marketing support to take up entrepreneurial activities in new and emerging trades. At the same time, women's traditional skills such as knowledge of herbal plants, weaving, food processing or providing 'care' will be recognized and marketed.

6.6.12 Homes and Homesteads for Poor Women: Home ownership not only provides shelter but also serves as collateral in credit markets and increases social status and security in the event of natural or man-made disasters. As more than half the women workers in the unorganized, non-agricultural sector work from their own homes, a home is a productive and wealth-generating asset for millions of low-income women. There is well documented evidence to show that in both the urban and rural context, women's ownership of housing offers a vital form of security against poverty and enhances associated economic and social status. There are three main sources of access to land: family, state and market. The challenge in the Eleventh Plan is to tap all these three sources. With the amendment of the Hindu Succession Act we have already taken the first step towards enhancing women's claims through inheritance. This should be strengthened by enacting gender-equal laws, adopting vigilance in recording women's claims, increasing legal awareness, and providing legal aid. All housing provided by the government during the Eleventh Plan should either be half in the name of the woman in the household or in the single name of the woman. Single women, widows and women in difficult circumstances will be given priority. Finally, the Eleventh Plan agenda will strive to support women's access via banks by developing a system of reaching housing finance at reasonable rates to poor women. This will require provision of subsidised credit, changes in land tenure policies and in norms for mortgages and housing loans.

6.6.13 Self-Help Groups: While strengthening SHG initiatives, policies and schemes in the Eleventh Plan will simultaneously increase women's awareness, bargaining power, literacy, health, vocational and entrepreneurial skills. It will prioritize training, capacity building inputs and the creation of backward/forward linkages, which are essential to generate sustainable livelihood opportunities. Given the scale of the phenomenon, there is a need to review the SHG interventions and the ground level realities to determine how SHGs may better serve the interests of poor women, and suggest changes required in overall SHG policy frameworks.

The Eleventh Plan recognizes the importance of this issue and proposes a High Level Committee to conduct a review of SHG related policies and programmes.

6.6.14 Social Empowerment: Healthcare access remains low for many women, especially the poor and marginalized who suffer from multiple exclusions and stigmatized groups such as sex workers and women with alternative sexualities. The Plan recognizes the gender dimension of health problems and seeks to address issues of women's survival and health through a life cycle approach. Making ordinary women partners in their own healthcare is an underpinning of Women's Health in the Eleventh Plan.

The Eleventh Plan agenda is to move beyond the traditional focus on family planning and reproductive health, to adopt a holistic perspective on women's health. For this, allocation towards health is being stepped up.

The high rates of MMR and IMR, poor pre natal and post natal care, combined with the low proportion of institutional deliveries is a grave cause of concern. Empowering adolescent girls through information about health, sexuality, and increased awareness to negotiate rights with families, future partners and in the workplace is equally important. The challenge is to create an enabling environment with information, services and health programmes for women to exercise their rights and choices.

Many other factors affect the health of women. For instance women's risk of mortality from indoor air pollution resulting from use of unprocessed fuels is estimated to be 50 percent higher than of men. While over time, community investment in low cost clean fuel such as biogas will be encouraged, in the interim, firewood needs to be made available. Provision of clean drinking water and sanitation facilities are also important for good health. Inter sectoral convergence to ensure the health and well being of women in this regard is a major challenge before the Eleventh Plan.

6.6.15 Political Empowerment: Notable constitutional,

legislative and policy reforms, and continued administrative decentralization have demonstrated the government's commitment to increase women's grassroots political participation. Although only one-third of seats were reserved for women by the 73rd and 74th constitutional amendments, the actual representation is higher at all levels. Women's increased political participation has yielded a range of positive results, not only for women, but also for their families and communities.

Central issues in development such as health, nutrition, family income and education are finding their way to the top of the agenda for action. Women's participation brings about more inclusive governance and effective community-centred development. Yet in many places, especially in states like UP, Bihar and Rajasthan, women continue to serve as proxies. The challenge for the Eleventh Plan is to ensure that women panchayat members are empowered to take their own decisions.

The Eleventh Plan will undertake the following measures to accelerate the process of women's political empowerment and participation in PRIs:

1. The no-confidence clause is often used to remove women sarpanches. State governments will be advised to ensure that women sarpanchs cannot be removed for at least a year and a half by a no-confidence motion. If a no-confidence vote is passed, the replacing incumbent should also be a woman from the same social group as the earlier incumbent;
2. States should revisit the two-child norm laws which prevent those who have more than two children from holding office. This law has been repealed across some states because it was found to be used against women and it disproportionately impacted poor, SC, ST, Muslim and Tribals. More tragically, the norm led to increasing female foeticide;
3. Increase resource allocation for capacity building of all

PRI members (male and female) in diverse areas pertaining to gender sensitization and women's rights, as well as in the political skill-building of women members of PRIs;

4. Greater effort to include poor and other excluded women on State Planning Boards and Commissions;
5. Funds for time-series evaluations of the impact of women on PRIs, and on enabling policy conditions and contextual factors for women's political participation;
6. Accelerate the State Governments' process of devolution and decentralization of powers, so that PRIs are not handicapped in carrying out their mandated duties.

6.6.16 Effective Implementation of Women Related Legislations: During the Tenth Plan period, some important legislations have been passed and amended. For example, besides the Hindu Succession (Amendment) Act 2005 and Protection of Women from Domestic Violence Act 2005 (PWDVA) mentioned earlier, the Dowry Prohibition Act was reviewed. A very active civil society has been relentlessly campaigning on these issues. Their experiences and recommendations will be taken on board to ascertain that the rights of every woman are enshrined in laws.

Under the Eleventh Plan budgetary allocations will be made for publicity and for creating the required infrastructure for effective implementation of these legislations. M/o WCD will appoint Protection Officers and setup district level cells to be responsible for monitoring and implementation of PWDVA and other Acts under its charge.

Ministry of WCD will also try and ensure the enactment of other legislations that benefit women. The Government is already contemplating the unorganized sector bill to provide social security to unorganized sector workers; schemes for life and health insurance have already been introduced. These should be implemented with a special emphasis on safeguarding the interests of women. The Dowry Prohibition Act (DPA) will be reviewed to clarify existing provisions relating to the definition of the dowry and penalties for guilty parties. Implementation of PWDVA with DPA will be linked to enable PWDVA protection officers to take action under the DPA. The Eleventh Plan will also have provisions for sensitization of medical professionals on recording of evidence in cases of dowry deaths, training and capacity building of law enforcement functionaries and awareness generation about problems of dowry. Efforts will be made to ensure effective monitoring and enforcement of PC and PNDT Act through Central and State Supervisory Boards and adequate allocation of funds. Public awareness and community mobilization will be generated along with training the authorities to deal with the issue of sex determination and sex selective abortions.

The M/o WCD will ensure the enactment of the Bill to prevent sexual harassment at the workplace. The Prevention of Immoral Trafficking Act is already being reviewed to ensure that women in prostitution are not victimised further. In addition to this, the Eleventh Plan will strengthen interregional networks to check forced migration and trafficking. Special police officers will be appointed to promote community level vigilance to reduce trafficking. There will be special training modules on trafficking for police, judiciary, and other government personnel. More rehabilitation homes will be established.

To tackle the conflict-related VAW, the Eleventh Plan will ensure the inclusion of provisions of sexual violence in the draft law on the prevention of communal violence. It will look into setting up Special Courts to deal with cases of VAW in conflict situations, including those involving security personnel. It will encourage women's involvement in peace keeping, community dialogues and conflict resolution. There will be special measures for compensation, financial assistance, and support to widows and female headed households in conflict areas.

The Eleventh Plan will foster women's access to legal services through a range of measures. Women will be exempted from paying fees to fight cases of human rights violations. Funds for legal assistance will be provided to poor women seeking legal redress. Legal awareness programmes will be carried out in all States in collaboration with NGOs working at the grassroots level. Legal Aid Cells consisting of committed and gender sensitive lawyers will be set up at the Panchayat level to provide information and support to rural women, especially poor women. Lok Adalats will be organized to encourage alternate dispute settlement mechanisms for efficacious settlement of cases. The Plan will also work towards increasing the percentage of women in police and judicial services. Training on use of gender specific laws will be provided to all Members and Authorities involved in providing legal services. Concept of Jan Sunwaiye will be adopted to listen to people's voices.

6.6.17 Gender Mainstreaming and Strengthening Delivery Mechanisms: In the Eleventh Plan, institutional mechanisms will carry forward the process of gender mainstreaming and will be strengthened. National Commission for Women (NCW) and State Commissions for Women will be strengthened to enable them to effectively play their role as the nodal agencies for the protection of rights of women. Towards this end, efforts will be made in the Eleventh plan to suitably amend the NCW Act to give the Commission more powers. The states likewise, will be urged to review the powers of their Women's Commissions. In addition to this, more functional and financial autonomy and a statutory base will have to be ensured for these organisations to strengthen their legal status. This will not only ensure that these bodies remain non-partisan, it will also increase their credibility.

A mechanism will be created to periodically report to the National Development Council the progress on Women's Plans with respect to the National Policy for Empowerment of Women. Action Plans for Women's Empowerment at national and state levels will be drawn up in consultation with all sectoral agencies and civil society including women's groups, lawyers, activists, women's study centres etc. Cross cutting issues such as unpaid work, land and asset entitlements, skill development and vocational training, child care, occupational health, wages, violence against women will be mainstreamed. Parivarik Mahila Lok Adalats will be organized, which will supplement the efforts of District Legal Service Authority (DLSA). Resource Centres for women will be set up at national and state levels and linked with Women's Study Centres.

Gender budgeting and Gender outcome assessment will be encouraged in all Ministries/Departments at Central and State levels. Gender Budgeting helps assess the gender differential impact of the budget and takes forward the translation of gender commitments to budgetary allocations. During the Eleventh Plan efforts will continue to create gender budgeting cells in all ministries and departments. Data from these cells will be collated on a regular basis and made available in the public domain.

Gender outcome assessment of fund flows has been made a mandatory part of the outcome budget prepared by every ministry/department as part of their budget documents. In 2005-06, this exercise covered 10 Departments and the total magnitude of the Gender Budget (i.e. women specific allocations) was recorded at 4.8 percent of total Union Government expenditure. In 2006-07, 24 Departments of the Union Government were included and the magnitude of the Gender Budget was 3.8 percent of total budget estimates. It was found that schemes, which do not have a 100 percent women's component also found a mention as women specific schemes. The Eleventh Plan will therefore ensure that each Ministry/Department of both Centre and State should put in place a systematic and comprehensive monitoring and auditing mechanism for outcome assessment. In addition, the Ministry of WCD, Ministry of Finance and Planning Commission will facilitate national level gender outcome assessments through spatial mapping of gender gaps and resource gaps. They will undertake gender audits of public expenditure, programmes, and policies and ensure the collection of standardized, gender disaggregated data (including data disaggregated for SC/ST and Minority women) at national, state and district levels.

In the Eleventh Plan period, the existing system of gender based planning will be extended to other Ministries and Departments and not confined only to those, which have historically been perceived as "women-related". Ministries and Departments such as Education, Health and Family Welfare, Agriculture, Rural Development, Labour, Tribal Affairs, Social Justice and Empowerment which have the potential to exceed the 30 percent WCP requirement will be encouraged to administer more women related programmes. During the Eleventh Plan, efforts will be made to extend the concept of gender based plan component to PRIs and to the 29 subjects transferred to them under the 73rd Constitutional Amendment. Recognizing that some women suffer greater deprivation and discrimination than others, the Eleventh Plan will refine the norms of WCP to prioritize the most vulnerable as beneficiaries, particularly SC, ST women, Muslim women, single women, differently-abled and HIV positive women, among others.

The Eleventh Plan period will also seek to engender all national policies and programmes right from their inception and formulation stages. The Ministry of Women and Child Development is the nodal Ministry for gender budgeting and the coordination mechanism for Gender Budgeting will ensure that all policies including fiscal and monetary policies, agricultural policies, non-farm sector, information and technology policies, public policy on migration, health insurance schemes, disaster management policies, media policy, and the legal regime among others are relevant from a gender perspective and are thoroughly examined. It will ensure that all legislations before they are presented to Parliament for enactment are cleared by the Parliamentary Committee on Women's Empowerment.

The Eleventh Plan is committed to ensuring the participation of women in governance through the smooth passage of the much-delayed Women's Reservation Bill. There will be simultaneous training and inputs for women in the PRIs to enable them to influence gender sensitive local planning and implementation. Gender disaggregated data on the participation of women, especially SC/ST and minority women, in Parliament, state legislative assemblies, Council of Ministers, premier services, and in the overall government sector will be collected and made available in the public domain. The Plan will also make pro-active efforts to provide competitive exam training and prioritize recruitment of women to All India Services especially IAS, IFS and IPS.

The M/o WCD will take the lead in creating and maintaining a comprehensive gender-disaggregated data base, for quantitative and qualitative data. The purpose would be (i) to base new initiatives on facts and figures, (ii) assess the gender impact of programmes and (iii) assess the level of women's participation in planning and implementing programmes.

6.6.18 Eleventh Plan Schemes: An integrated scheme for women's empowerment through Self Help Groups (SHGs) will be the major scheme to be implemented by the Ministry of WCD in the Eleventh Plan. Swayamsidha Phase-II will be launched as a countrywide programme with larger coverage in states lagging behind in women development indices. The lessons learnt from Swayamsiddha Part 1 and Swashakti, especially regarding capacity building of poor women through Self Help Groups, promoting thrift and credit activities amongst the women themselves, emphasising on participatory approach towards poverty alleviation, and addressing common problems and issues through the SHGs, will be incorporated in the universalized Swayamsidha.

Support to Training and Employment Programme (STEP), a scheme for skill training of women, will be revamped during the Eleventh plan based on evaluation results (under way) and will be integrated with Swayamsidha to ensure adequate outlay for country wide implementation as a Centrally Sponsored Scheme. The Rashtriya Mahila Kosh will also be integrated with STEP and Swayamsidha for credit linkages, but will be reviewed in the Eleventh Plan period before considering any further expansion.

A separate Women Empowerment and Livelihood Project assisted by IFAD will be implemented during the Eleventh Plan in four districts of U.P and two districts of Bihar.

Various social empowerment schemes for women will be implemented during the Eleventh Plan. Condensed Courses of Education will be run to facilitate skill development and vocational training of adult girls and women who could not join mainstream education system or were forced to dropout from formal schools. This will improve their social and economic status by making them employable. The Ministry will use mass media to run an Awareness Generation Project on issues relating to the status, rights and problems of women. Through this project it will also try to ensure a balanced portrayal of women in newspapers, media channels, serials, films etc.

The most important programme for women to be run by the Ministry of WCD during the Eleventh Plan will be the provision of maternity benefits. The ICDS scheme will have a component of conditional maternity benefits under which pregnant and lactating mothers will be entitled to cash incentives for 3 months before birth and 3 months after the birth of the child. This will encourage and enable mothers to avoid physically stressful activities, meet medical and nutrition supplementation expenses during the last trimester and spend time with the child after birth. The benefits under the scheme will be conditional to the mother being registered with the Anganwadi, having regular health check up and immunization.

Ministry of WCD will continue to run its schemes offering support services. Under a revised Working Women's Hostel scheme, financial assistance will be provided to NGOs, cooperative bodies and other agencies for construction/renting of buildings for hostels to provide safe and affordable accommodations to working women. The scheme of Swadhar Homes for destitute women and women in difficult circumstance will continue, albeit with modifications. A women's helpline foundation will also be set up. Under the Short-stay Home scheme, suitable accommodation with basic amenities and services like counselling, legal aid, medical facilities, vocational training and rehabilitation will be provided for women and girls who are victims of marital conflict, crime or homelessness.

The Central Social Welfare Board (CSWB) will continue financing NGOs for implementation of various women and child related schemes. But during the Plan, all the existing schemes of the CSWB will be reviewed and restructured in the light of current requirements. If necessary, some of them will also be merged with schemes of WCD.

7

Training and Motivation of Women Entrepreneurs

7.1 Introduction

The future belongs to real entrepreneurs, those competent and capable to meet the coming challenges of increased competition, decline of protected markets, new technologies and foreign collaboration. Those who have necessary entrepreneurial, managerial capabilities and skills would find liberalization full of opportunities for expansion and growth while those who survived so far because of large margins provided by the imperfect market conditions would complain about liberalization and succumb to the pressures. Only option they have is to wake up to the needs to strengthen their personal capabilities and thereby become better entrepreneurs than they have been so far.

Education is a strong interventional or influencing media that sets values, develops attitudes and creates drive in people to move in professional and vocational direction with confidence. Values, attitudes and motivation combined together propel masses to acquire skills and competencies to achieve the goals directed by values which are mostly acquired at an early education stage. In the present era when there are ample opportunities and increasing need for entrepreneurship, the short supply of entrepreneurs in the society is largely because of the absence of entrepreneurship element in the education system. In spite of massive investment made in the successive Five Year Plans, the actual impact on the life of the common people in the remote area has been comparatively limited. It is for this reason that administrators and planners are slowly beginning to realize that monetary assistance and infrastructural facilities are necessary but not sufficient conditions for economic/industrial growth and that the human factor will remain significant. There is need to develop a sound conceptual base for evolving the curriculum which can be used for the emergence of entrepreneurial spirit including values, attitudes, motivation and competences among masses at a very early stage of their development to successfully take up the entrepreneurial pursuits.

The chemistry of a true entrepreneur's mind is thus characterized by an enterprise which manifests itself in his risk taking behaviour, shaped in the background, by his inherent achievement motivation. But, achievement motivation alone does not make a good entrepreneur. Achievement motivation, for effective entrepreneurship, must be ideally blended with the inclination to do something independently and that, too, for the good of the society where the society factor is represented by the owner stakeholder's interests in the business enterprise, where the constituents are: the customers, the employees, the suppliers, the neighbourhood, the state, the nation and so on.

7.2 Emphasis on Women Entrepreneurship Development

A country's economic progress is found to be positively correlated with the rise in number and quality of its entrepreneurs. The entrepreneur as the determining factor in the creation of new wealth in society has since been recognized.

The economic policies of the Government of India clearly emphasis the emergence of Women Entrepreneurship purely from the economic perspective, according to which, creating a favourable economic-politico environment with support systems would lead to Women Entrepreneurship among men and women. Slowly but surely women have begun to chip away one of the last and most enduring bastions of male dominance.

Traditionally it was believed that Entrepreneurs are born and not made, but researchers and practitioners are eager to facilitate and accelerate the process of Entrepreneurship and conducted research and experiments on Entrepreneurship and came to the conclusion that Entrepreneurship is not solely an inherent quality, but that it can also be developed and encouraged in individuals.

It has been recognized that in the development of Women Entrepreneurship the crucial factor besides, individual, social, economic, and organizational factors, as it is the individual who has to perceive and respond to these other factors to become an entrepreneur, therefore, the focus is on the individual- the potential entrepreneur in the entrepreneurial development programmes. It is being increasingly felt that a potential entrepreneur, before he decides to set up his enterprise ought to be equipped with the necessary enterprise building and enterprise management skills, besides being highly achievement oriented, and thus, the entrepreneurial development programmes gained importance and momentum, particularly in India and in other developing countries.

7.3 Emphasis on Small Enterprise Development

The 1990s was foreseen as the decade of entrepreneurial explosion in India and it was felt that Women Entrepreneurship is going to be the focal point of development in the next two Five Year Plans. Be it the problem of unemployment, income generation, increasing GNP, regional imbalance in industrial progress, Women Entrepreneurship seems to be the potential answer. The New Industrial Policy stated that the small scale industrial sector has emerged as a dynamic and vibrant sector of the economy during the 1980s. The primary objective of the Small Scale Industrial Policy during the 1990s would be to import more vitality and growth-impetus to the sector to enable it to contribute its mite fully to the economy, particularly in terms of growth output, employment and exports. Thus, it seems that the government view industry, specifically, Women Entrepreneurship and small scale sector, as one of the saviours of the sagging economy, high inflation etc., and therefore, there is all the more reason that Women Entrepreneurship should be encouraged and promoted as they constitute over 48 percent of the population of India.

The importance of industrial enterprises in the development of women needs no introduction. The prevalent social structures of today, because of historical reasons, have prevented the balanced development of women along with men. In fact, what is sought for as a remedy is to provide positively discriminatory opportunities for women along with men. Such opportunities are expected to generate some capabilities among women, which in turn, may help them to reproduce such capabilities.

Two streams of thought have influenced the promotion of Women Entrepreneurship in India by the government as well as by various other agencies. The first stream is employment centred. It has been argued that, considering their weaker bargaining power in society, women should be given higher priority in entrepreneurial schemes. The second stream of thought relates to the argument for autonomy of women. The argument is that, with an assumed equal status with men in society, there should be strong efforts to develop Women Entrepreneurship on par with those of men.

Development policy for the women enterprises, just as in the case of other enterprises, should take serious attention towards maximum usage of backward linkages and concentration in areas where women have a greater potential for developing and sustaining them. Similarly, the forward linkages also should be taken care of. In fact, such permissive sequence is often found very negligible in the case of most such enterprises. In fact, considering the higher vulnerability of women enterprises, it is important that this added dimension is introduced as a component of public policy.

There is a realization that full involvement of women in small enterprise development would ensure effective utilization of all available labour and improve for quality of life. This leads to the presumption that action must be taken by the governments to analyse current status and potential role of women in the process of industrialization with a view to bring positive change which would result in sharing of responsibilities and benefits by both sexes.

Self-employment was encouraged by providing a package of services such as training, credit, marketing and general guidance for those who desired to launch self-employment venture. Requisite information and facilities were provided with the help of on-window approach. Of late, a number of organized attempts have been made to help groom women as potential entrepreneurs.

7.4 Training and Motivating of Women Entrepreneurs

The training programme should sub-serve the following objectives:

- To impart basic knowledge about the industry, product and production methods;
- To build the necessary skills of new Women Entrepreneurs and workers;
- To assist the women entrepreneur/worker to function more effectively in her present position by exposing him to the latest concept, techniques and information;
- To build up second line of workers and prepare them to shoulder additional responsibility and/or switch on to the production of a new product, if there is any diversification;
- To expose the women entrepreneur to the latest developments which directly or indirectly affect him;
- To broaden the vision of Women Entrepreneurs by providing them suitable opportunities for an interchange of experiences within and outside an industry;
- To impart customer education; and
- To impart knowledge about the marketing of goods.

Apart from the above, the objectives of entrepreneurial training are:

- To let the women entrepreneur set or reset the objectives of her business and work individually and along with her group for their realization.

- To prepare her for accepting totally unforeseen risks of business after such training.
- To enable her to take strategic decisions.
- To enable her to build an integrated team to fulfil the demands of tomorrow.
- To communicate fast, clearly and effectively.
- To develop a broad vision to see the business as a whole and to integrate her function with it.
- To enable her to relate her product and industry to the total environment, to find what is significant in it and to take it into account in her decisions and actions.
- To enable her to cope with and coordinate all relevant paper work, most of which is statutorily obligatory.
- To strengthen her integrity, honestly and compliance with law, the key to success in the long run.

7.5 Inter-agency Co-operation

- National Small Industries Corporation (NSIC), Small Industries Development Organization (SIDO), Khadi and Village Industries Commission (KVIC), Handloom Board, Silk Board, Commodity Boards etc. have schemes to help SSI units is completing their products. Some of them also help in promoting exports of goods manufactured by SSI Units/Entrepreneurs.
- SIDO is one of the important agencies that help SSI units in marketing their product through consultancy, testing and marketing facilities. The SIDO functions as nodal agency for formulating, coordinating and monitoring policies and programmes for promotion and development of small scale industries of the country.
- SIDCO also promotes ancillary units to public sector enterprises. Besides, any large industrial houses actively pursuit the policy of promoting ancillary units for their purchases of stores. SSI units can take advantage of this facility and secure a regular market for their products.

- District Industries Centres (DICs) provide marketing and other assistance to SSI under a single roof.
- State-level Small Industries Corporation (SICs) participates in tender programmes or government purchases and then sub-contracts these tenders to SSI units.
- The Government of India has established trade centres at various places which disseminate information on market potentials and conditions. These centres also organize fairs and exhibitions where SSI units can exhibit and sell their products.
- Twenty seven Small Industry Service Institutes (SISIs) have been set up by SIDO at various places for disseminating market information. Thirty Eight Exchange Centres have also been set up within some SISIs to help units in securing sub-contract jobs.
- The Small Scale Industrial sector raises term credit and working capital required by it from commercial banks, cooperative banks and State Financial Corporations.
- The SIDO has already set up 31 branches of Small Industries Service Institutes, 4 Regional Testing Centres, 3 Process cum Product Development Centres and 20 Field Testing Stations to provide a comprehensive range of facilities to small scale units.
- The specialized institutes like Central Institute of Tool Design, Hyderabad, Central Tool Room and Training Centres at Ludhiana and Calcutta, Central Institute of Hand Book, Jalandhar. Institute of Design of Electrical Measuring Instrument (IDEMI) Mumbai. Integrated Trading Centre, Nilokhen. National Institute of Small Industry Extension Training, Hyderabad, National Institute for Women Entrepreneurship and Small Businessman Development, New Delhi conduct specialized courses and job oriented training programs for the benefit of small scale industries.

7.6 Effectiveness of Programmes/Courses

Further, the Women Entrepreneurs should be able to undertake the following:

- Develop and strengthen their entrepreneurial quality/motivation;
- Analyse environment related to small enterprise, and small business;
- Select project/product;
- Formulate projects;
- Understand the process and procedure of setting up of small enterprise;
- Know and influence the source of help support needed for launching the enterprise;
- Acquire the basic management skills;
- Know the pros and cons of being an entrepreneur; and
- Acquaint and appreciate the needed social responsibility/ entrepreneurial disciplines.

7.7 Methodology of Training

The following are the important methods by which training may be imparted:

- Individual instruction: Under this method, a single individual is selected for training. This mode of training is undertaken where a complicated skill is to be taught to an individual.
- Group instruction: This mode of training is suitable for a group of individuals with a similar type of work and where general instructions are applicable to all are to be given.
- Lecture method: Here the instructor communicates in theory the practice to be followed by the learners. Under this method, whenever there are any doubts, they may be clarified on the spot.
- Demonstration method: where the performance of work is to be shown practically by the instructor for better understanding, this method can be followed. This is more concerned with the practical than theoretical aspect.

- Written instructional method: The medium of training is followed where a future reference is to be made by the learners. This method is mostly followed where a standardized production system is followed.
- Conference: Conferences are frequently organized wherein experts in the field share their ideas and bring to the notice of learners new ideas and techniques to increase production.
- Meetings: Meetings are a mode of training involving a group of people who discuss the various problems confronting them. They involve exchanging ideas and views and later on, coming to a firm conclusion based on the various proposals and alternatives.

The Women Entrepreneurship Development movement is primarily based on the belief that people can accept Women Entrepreneurship as a career. In order to accelerate the speed of self employment and Women Entrepreneurship development, various institutions and organizations were established by the government, particularly during the Third Five Year Plan. These institutions and organizations cater to the business needs and requirements of the entrepreneurs. Particularly, the 'first generation entrepreneurs' is the focal point.

7.8 Motivation of Women Entrepreneurs

Motivation plays an important role in starting an enterprise. This is the impelling force which draws a woman out of her house and inspires her to start something on her own. Special motivation schemes/incentives, single window facilities, better and easier financial facilities, dissemination of information, simplified procedures and rules, special cell to look into the problems and difficulties of Women Entrepreneurs and directives from the government will improve the participation of the women.

An essential element in the entrepreneur's approach to risk taking situations is the willingness to accept personal responsibility for the consequences of the decision, regardless of whether the consequences are favourable or unfavourable. Other persons find it difficult to accept personal responsibility for decisions which may lead to failure, and they often attribute events in their lives to luck or to forces beyond their control, such as competition with big business or government interference.

Most entrepreneurial traits are inter-related. This is particularly so with risk-taking behaviour.

- Risk-taking is related to creativity and innovation, and it is an essential part in turning ideas into reality.
- Risk-taking is related to self-confidence. The more confidence you have in your own abilities, the greater confidence you will have in being able to affect the outcome of your decisions and a greater willingness to take what others see at risks.
- Realistic knowledge of your own capabilities is also important. Such realism serves to restrict your activities to situation in which you can affect the outcomes.

7.9 Identification of Potential Women Entrepreneurs

Identification of entrepreneurs has been operationalised as the activity of initial discrimination and screening from amongst the universe. Activities in pre-selection stage reflect the process of discrimination in a multi-stage identification technique. The multi-stage operation helps in arriving at the target group, logically and very rationally. The pre-selection programming is aimed at structuring the application blank for initial screening of entrepreneur with a very logical and rational way of rejecting or selecting a person.

A multi stage discrimination process would enable to pinpoint the potential target group before the training and follow-up stages. A logical rating or weightage has to be decided, well in advance by the development agency. Identification process has to be initiated right from the advertisement stage to discriminate the potential and non-potential candidates with the support of development or linkage agencies who are involved in this programme. The nature of advertisement would attract and distract the attention of genuine or neo-entrepreneurs respectively.

7.10 Selection of Potential Women Entrepreneurs

The entrepreneur identification and selection mechanism which precedes training is based on the following key assumptions:

- Not everybody can become an entrepreneur as an entrepreneur must have certain traits.
- Such traits are identifiable and measurable through some psychological and behavioural tests supported by social indices.
- People possessing these traits or showing evidence of these traits can be developed to acquire necessary dimensions of Women Entrepreneurship.

This had led to a 3-step selection process which begins with preliminary screening of those responding to the intensive promotional effort undertaken in the location by the Trainer/Motivator. A specially devised form which screens out those with only a casual interest in the programme is used for this purpose. This is followed by an assessment of a candidate's entrepreneurial trait level by applying behavioural science techniques. The process ends with individual interviews for overall assessment about a candidate's suitability to undertake manufacturing activity or business, together with an understanding of his specific needs for training.

The entrepreneurial traits assessed in the course of behavioural tests include:

- The need to achieve: This can be seen in an individual's desire to compete with some standard of excellence and success in performance.
- Risk-taking: Women Entrepreneurs are found to have an inclination to take calculated, moderate, intelligent risks.

They tend to avoid extremes of both easy and risky situations.

- Positive Self Concept: Includes self-confidence as well as self-efficacy and a positive image of one's abilities and achievements.
- Initiative and Independence: Such people not only show initiative but also independence in their day-to-day behaviour. They like to act on their own rather than follow directions.
- Problem-solving: A tendency to approach problems in order to solve them.
- Hopeful about future: Despite of dissatisfaction with present working conditions.
- An interest in environment scanning: To seek answers to present questions.
- Urge for goal setting and time-bound planning: With desire to fulfil time bound plans.[11]

7.11 Guidance of Women Entrepreneurs

Women Entrepreneurs need guidance regarding the following aspects.

1. Identification and Selection of Product- A woman entrepreneur is an opportunity seeker and the first major decision that she has to take is the selection of the right business opportunity. Opportunities exist is any environment, but Women Entrepreneurs can be made more aware of them and be helped to identify and select a viable product or service idea in a given environment.
2. Preparation of project plan- Before launching a new venture, the woman entrepreneur needs to study the feasibility of the new product by conducting a market survey. Instead of directly working on the business plan, a market survey is advisable as it will help in assessing the potential of the product, and only then the business plans should be prepared. The following aspects need to be explained in detail to the potential and existing women

entrepreneurs.

- Assessing feasibility of a product, technical, financial, marketing and commercial;
- Assessing market potential;
- Determining the size of unit and investment;
- Working capital estimation;
- Choosing appropriate technology, infrastructure and staff requirements;
- Financial calculations, fund and cash flow;
- Calculating cost of production and profitability.

3. Consolidation of Resources-Potential Women Entrepreneurs should understand the existing problems and the environment under which they will work to initiate the enterprise. They need to develop and strengthen awareness building and understanding the peculiarities and problems of women entrepreneurs, finding resources of information, knowing the prevailing government policies and incentives essential for enterprise creation and understanding the procedural requirement for setting up business/industry.

7.12 Adequacy of Skills to Impart Training

Potential Women Entrepreneurs require the motivation necessary to sustain their efforts and commitment while implementing their plans and operating their enterprise. One of the main characteristics of an entrepreneur is the need to achieve; this enables the Women Entrepreneurs to set realistic goals on the basis of self analysis, as well as an awareness of one's strengths and weaknesses. The trainers should have the following skills to help the women to analyse and clarify the demands arising from their new identity as entrepreneurs.

7.12.1 Conceptualising Entrepreneurial and Behavioural Skills: The focus of Women Entrepreneurship Development is on the woman as an entrepreneur. Therefore, her potential has to be identified, tapped, energised and ultimately her vision transformed into action. Experiential learning situations (simulations, games, etc.) have to be created to help the potential entrepreneur to examine her own attitude towards Women Entrepreneurship and to give her an opportunity to practice the newly learnt behaviour and attitudes.

7.12.2 Learning and Practicing Entrepreneurial Behavioural Skills: Specialised training skills should be possessed by trainers to develop these competencies, among women entrepreneurs. They are:

- Initiative taking: The woman entrepreneur takes actions that go beyond job requirements or the demands of the situation;
- Sees and Acts on opportunities: She looks for and takes action on opportunities;
- Persistence: She takes repeated actions to meet a challenge or overcome an obstacle;
- Information Seeking: She personally seeks information on markets, customers, suppliers, competitors, technology etc.
- Concern for Quality, Innovation and Efficiency: She takes action to meet or extend standards of excellence, and improves on past performance and has an overall commitment to the work contract;
- Systematic Planning: She develops and uses logical step by step plans to reach her goals by breaking a large task into sub tasks;
- Problem Solving: She generates new and potentially unique ideas or innovative solutions to reach the goals;
- Self-Confidence: She has a strong belief in her own abilities;
- Persuasion and Influencing Strategies: She uses a variety of strategies to influence or persuade others so as to accomplish her set objectives;
- Goal Setting: She articulates long range vision and goals. She continuously sets, monitors and revises short range objectives.
- Risk Taking: She takes personal responsibility, welcomes

challenges and takes calculated and moderate risks.

7.13 Preparation of Feasibility Report

Project report is prepared mainly with the idea of obtaining bank finance rather than with a view to guiding future operations the entrepreneur gets the report prepared by a consultant. As such, financial corporations and commercial banks providing term loans are the parties interested in project report because it spells out how production should be organised to yield maximum results.

7.13.1 Project Idea: The project idea is examined in the context of internal and external constraints. At this stage there could only be three entrepreneurs. First time project idea seems to be feasible, second, the project idea is not a feasible, and third, unable to arrive at a conclusion for want of adequate data. If it is feasible, we proceed to the second step, if not feasible, we abandon the idea and if sufficient data is not available, we make efforts to collect the required data and design development.

7.13.2 Techno Economic Analysis: In this step, estimation of project demand potential and choice of optimal technology are made. The project may produce goods or services; it is imperative to know the market for such goods or services produced. Market analysis is also in built in this step. The choice of technology itself will be based on the demand potential and aid in project design. Techno-economic analysis gives to the project an individually and sets the stage for detailed design development.

7.13.3 Project Design and Network Analysis: This is an important step in project formulation since this step defines individual activities which constitute the project and their inter relationship with each other. The sequence of events of the project is presented. A detailed work plan and the project is prepared with time allocation for each activity and presented in a network drawing Project design is the heart of the project entity. This paves the way for detailed identification and quantification of the project inputs an essential step in the development of the financial and cost benefit profile of the project.

7.13.4 Input Analysis: This step assesses the input requirements during the construction of the project and also during the operation of the project. A project was divided into several activities. Now it is better to see to the inputs required for each activity and sum it up to get at the total input requirements. Inputs assessment should be in qualitative and quantitative terms. Inputs include materials as well as human resources. Input analysis also considers the recurring as well as non-recurring resource requirements of the project and evaluate the feasibility of the project from the point of view of the availability of these resources. Inputs assessment will aid in assessing the cost of the project itself which in turn is necessary for financial analysis or cost benefit analysis.

7.13.5 Financial Analysis: This stage mainly involves estimating the project costs, estimating the project operating costs and project fund requirements. Financial analysis also helps in comparing the various project proposals on a common scale, thereby aiding the decision

The purpose of financial analysis is to present some measures to assess the financial viability of the project. A proforma balance sheet for the project data should be performed. Depreciation should be allowed for on the basis specified by the Bureau of Public Enterprises Foreign Exchange requirements should be cleared by the Department of Economic Affairs. The feasibility report should take into account income tax rebates for priority industries, incentives for backward areas, accelerated depreciation etc. The sensitivity analysis should also be presented. The report must analyze the sensitivity of the rate of return of change in the level and pattern of product prices.

7.13.6 Cost Benefit Analysis: The overall worth of project is the main consideration here. While financial analysis will try to justify a project from the profitability point of view.

Here again, the project design forms the basis of evaluation. When we talk of cost-benefit analysis, we not only take into account the direct costs and direct benefits of the project but also the costs which all entities connected with the project have to bear and the benefits which will be enjoyed by all such entities. The idea here is to evaluate the project in terms of apparent costs and benefits. Cost benefit analysis is an integrated technique in assessing the viability of a project, while keeping a close eye on costs. Cost benefit analysis is not the internationally recognised system of project formulation.

7.13.7 Pre-investment Analysis: The project proposal gets a formal and final shape at this stage. All the results obtained in the above steps are consolidated to present a total picture various conclusions arrived at are present. At this stage, the project is presented in such a way that the project sponsoring body, the project implementing body and the outside agencies will be able to decide whether to accept the proposal or not. The sum total of the pre investment appraisal is to present the project idea in a form in which the project sponsoring body, the project implementing body can take an investment decision regarding the project.

The feasibility report lies in between the project formulating stage and the appraisal and sanction stage. The project formulation stage involves the identification of investment options by the enterprise in consultation with the Administrative Ministry, the Planning Commission and other concerned authorities.

7.13.8 General Information: The feasibility report should include an analysis of the industry to which the project belongs. It should deal with the past performance of the industry. The description of the type of industry should also be given, i.e. the priority of the industry, increase in production, role of the public sector, allocation of investment of funds, choice of technique, etc. This should also contain information about the enterprise submitting the feasibility report.

7.13.9 Preliminary Analysis of Alternatives: This should contain present data on the gap between demand and supply for the outputs which are to be produced, data on the capacity that would be available from projects that are in production or under implementation at the tune the report is prepared, a complete list of all existing plants in the industry, giving their capacity and level of production actually attained a list of all projects for which letters of intent/licenses have been issued and a list of proposed projects. All options that are technically feasible should be considered at this preliminary stage. The location of the project and as implications should also be looked into. An account of the foreign exchange requirement should be taken. The profitability of different options should also be given. The rate of return on investment should be calculated and presented in the report. Alternative cost calculations vis-à-vis return should be presented.

7.13.10 Project Description: The feasibility report should provide a brief description of the technology/process chosen for the project. Information relevant to determining the optimality of the location chosen should also be included. To assist in the assessment of the environmental effects of a project, every feasibility report must present the information on specific points, i.e., population, water, land, air, flora and fauna, effects arising out of project's pollution, other environmental disruption, etc. the report should contain a list of important items of capital equipment and also a list of the operational requirements of the plant, requirements of water and power, requirements of personnel organisational structure envisaged, transport costs, activity wise phasing of construction and factors affecting it.

7.13.11 Marketing Plan: It should contain the following items: Data on the marketing plan. Demand and prospective supply in each of the areas to be served. The methods and the data used for main estimates of domestic supply and selection of the market areas should be presented. Estimates of the degree of price sensitivity should be presented. It should contain an analysis of past trends in prices.

7.13.12 Capital Requirements and Costs: The estimates should be reasonably complete and properly estimated. Information on all items of costs should be carefully collected and presented.

7.13.13 Operating Requirements and Costs: Operating costs are essentially those costs, which are incurred after the commencement of commercial production. Information about all items of operating cost should be collected. Operating costs relate to the cost of raw materials and intermediates, fuel, utilities, labour, repair and maintenance, selling expenses and other expenses.

7.13.14 Economic Analysis: Social profitability analysis needs some adjustment in the data relating to the costs and returns to the enterprise. One important type of adjustment involves a correction in input and costs, to reflect the true value of foreign exchange, labour, and capital. The enterprise should try to assess the impact of its operations on foreign trade. Indirect costs and benefits should also be included in the report. If they cannot be quantified, they should be analyzed and their importance is emphasized.

7.14 Post-training Contact of Institutions

Post-training contact is needed at two levels and institutions have made themselves available for getting the desired results. Follow-up with Women Entrepreneurs refers to the support given in sustaining their motivation and in helping them prepare business plans, establish enterprises, develop operational and management skills to sustain the enterprise.

The second aspect is follow-up at institutional level means follow-up with financial and other support institutions to solve problems of the women pertaining to loan procurement and complying with formalities to get necessary sanctions for the resources they need to establish their enterprise such as procurement of raw materials, developing market linkages.

Women Entrepreneurship Development Programmes without proper post-training support are lacking an important component. The involvement of key personnel from the support agencies right from the beginning helps the women to get better support during the project implementation stage, and this in turn will make the trainer's job of follow-up easier. It is vital to formulate strategies for appropriate linkages by the women to obtain finance and other infrastructure support. The active involvement of financial institutions and banks during the training stages is advisable as it ensures their support and can yield positive results. The approach adopted for follow-up activities should not be to spoon-feed the women, but to provide support, guidance and counselling whenever necessary.

8

Institutions Engaged in Promoting Women Entrepreneurship

8.1 National Institute of Small Industry Extension

A conceptual model worked out by the National Institute of Small Industry Extension, Hyderabad, for development of entrepreneurship involves various activities, which may be grouped into three categories:

1. Stimulatory activities;
2. Support activities; and
3. Sustaining activities.

8.1.1 Stimulatory Activities: The stimulatory activities include entrepreneurial education, planned publicity about entrepreneurial opportunities, identification of potential entrepreneurs opportunities, identification of potential entrepreneurs in a give area, motivating them by providing economic insight and managerial skills through training, helping entrepreneurs select new products and develop feasibility reports, setting up local agencies with fully trained personnel for entrepreneurial motivation and counselling, creating forums of entrepreneurs to discuss their mutual problems and success, and finally creating conditions where entrepreneurs get due recognition. These stimulatory activities are intended to ensure emergence of entrepreneurs and to generate initial motivation.

The following are the stimulatory functions of the District Industries Centre. They are as follows:

- Publicity of entrepreneurship opportunities;
- Entrepreneurial Education;
- Identification of entrepreneurs;
- Motivation or training to prospective entrepreneurs;
- Implant training to entrepreneurs;

- Help and guidance in selecting the product;
- Preparing and evaluating the project
- Arranging techno-economic information to entrepreneurs;
- Making available the product profile;
- Evolving locally suitable and new product processes;
- Training officers for counselling and promotion of entrepreneurship;
- Offering entrepreneurial counselling;
- Organizing entrepreneurial forums; and
- Publishing journals useful to entrepreneurial development.

8.1.2 Support Functions:

- Registering the unit;
- Arranging finance on credit;
- Providing shed, power, water etc.;
- Help and guidance in selecting machinery and equipment;
- Supplying scarce raw material;
- Providing common facility centres;
- Assisting in quality control; and
- Offering managerial consultancy.

8.1.3 Sustaining Functions:

- Help in marketing of the product;
- Help in modernizing the unit;
- Help and guide in expanding the unit; and
- Help and guide in replacement of equipment [4].

It is proposed to examine the role of the institutions/agencies in the promotion of entrepreneurship in Andhra Pradesh, with special reference to district, in undertaking stimulatory, support and sustaining functions.

8.2 Directorate/Commissionerate of Industries

The Directorate of Industries is established at a state level under the Ministry of Industry, Power and Labour. The Development Commissioner is the head of the Directorate. He is assisted by the Additional Commissioner, Additional Director and Joint Directors. For the administrative purpose, the state is divided into Divisions/Zones.

Initially, all the functions related to promotion and development of new industries and small Women Entrepreneurs were assigned to the Directorate of Industries. But, to accelerate the speed of implementation of the scheme and enhance efficiency, the government has established separate corporations like SSIDC, IDC, SFC, etc. These corporations function under the directives of the Directorate of Industries.

8.3 District Industries Centre (DIC)

To initiate the process of industrial development in each district, the Central Government established District Industries Centres (DIC) in each district of the country. DIC functions under the Directorate of Industries. Each DIC is headed by a General Manager who is assisted by managers to look after the following activities.

- Economic Investigation
- Plant and Machinery
- Research, Education and Training
- Raw Materials
- Credit Facilities
- Marketing Assistance
- Cottage Industries

8.4 State Financial Corporations (SFCs)

Finance is another important factor of production. The easy availability of financial resources is an impetus for the speedy development of industries. Particularly, new Women Entrepreneurs have a severe problem of dearth of capital. To overcome this hurdle in the industrialization of the country, the government has established State Financial Corporations (SFC) in each state according to the provisions of "State Financial Corporation Act, 1951".

SFC is one of the pioneering corporations established to fulfil the financial needs of the small and medium scale industries. The prime objective of SFC is to cater to the long run financial requirements of the entrepreneurs. It gives long term loans for the purchase of fixed assets like land, building, machinery, and equipment. Loans are given for the new industrial units as well as for the modernization of the existing units. Loans are not given for the repayment of the working capital. Recently, SFC gives financial assistance for the repayment of working capital worth Rs. 10 lakh. For this purpose the total project cost limit is Rs. 20 lakh.

According to the SFC Act, loans are given to the industrial units engaged in manufacturing preservation of perishable products, mining, hotel industry, testing, repairing and assembly of any type of machinery and vehicles for the passengers and goods transport by road or by sea.

In the service industry sector, units engaged in activities like analytical and testing laboratories, repairing of television, repairing and maintenance of air-conditioners, computer services (excluding computer training classes), tourism related entertainment and cultural centres, hotels, tourism services, video recording studio, weighbridges, salt manufacturing, chicken meat production, stone crushing and coal manufacturing for domestic use.

Important aspects and conditions considered by SFC while scrutinizing the loan proposals are:

- Promoter's contribution
- Debt-Equity Ratio
- Margin
- Security and collateral security

8.5 Khadi and Village Industries Commission (KVIC)

As per the provisions of a Special Parliamentary Act 1956, the Government has established Khadi and Village Industries Commission.

8.5.1 Objectives of KVIC

- To preserve the traditional arts and crafts in India.
- To equip the artisans and craftsmen to take up the

challenges of the modern market

- To promote the handicrafts, khadi, village and cottage industry by facilitating them with the necessary inputs like raw materials, equipments, capital, etc.
- To develop a market for these products
- To introduce the products even in the international market

To achieve these objectives the following schemes are provided by KVIC.

- Financial assistance for purchase of land, building, workshop, shed machinery and equipment at 4 percent rate of interest
- Working capital provision
- Equip capital
- Loan provision for purchase of raw materials
- Marketing avenues and selling centres for the products of artisans and craftsmen
- Subsidies for the registered societies of artisans and craftsmen belonging to schedule castes scheduled tribes, ex-servicemen,, women, etc.

8.6 Small Industries Service Institute (SISI)

Small Industries Service Institute is a national level organization established by the Central Government. At the state level, SISI functions under the Director assisted by Deputy Directors.

8.7 National Small Industries Corporation (NSIC)

National Small Industries Development Corporation is a national level institution. It was set up as 1955 as a Central Government undertaking. The main aim of NSIC is to fulfil the requirement of machinery and equipment for the development of small entrepreneurs. It is observed that the constraint faced by the Women Entrepreneurs is the dearth of investible funds to purchase machinery and equipment. Dearth of finance deprives many new Women Entrepreneurs from entrepreneurial opportunities.

NSIC is established to cater to this need of the entrepreneur. NSIC provides plant, machinery and equipment on a hire purchase basis. Under its special scheme, Women Entrepreneurs can procure indigenous as well as imported machinery. But the scheme does not include second hand machinery and machinery costing less than Rs.1000. NSIC also assists the Women Entrepreneurs in procuring government orders for various items of stores. The prescribed application forms are available in all of NSIC, SISI and DICs. Depending upon the cost of the machinery, an entrepreneur has to pay an application fee of Rs. 50 to Rs. 1,000. The processing fee is 2 percent to 5 percent of the cost of the machinery. Service Fee depends upon the location of the unit. Discrimination is made between the units located in industrially developed regions and the units of scheduled castes, scheduled tribes, persons with disabilities, ex-servicemen and women. The cost of the machinery is to be repaid in 13 equal settlements. In some cases, the cost is to be repaid in 9 instalments. New Women Entrepreneurs are given social incentives. They can pay the first instalment after 18 months from the date of contract with NSIC. The rate of interest charged by NSIC is usually 16 to 21 percent. For imported machinery, an entrepreneur has to abide by the provisions of the import policy of the government. Women Entrepreneurs have to secure a license for such imports. In special cases, Women Entrepreneurs have to prepare prototypes of the machines.

8.8 Small Industries Development Bank of India (SIDBI)

Small Industries Development Bank of India was established in 1990 as a development has exclusively for the small scale industries. It is a Central Government undertaking. The prime act of SIDBI is to promote and develop small industries by providing them the valuable factors of production, finance. Many institutions and commercial banks supply finance, both long-term and short-term, to small entrepreneurs. SIDBI coordinates the work of all of them.

Financial Assistance Scheme of SIDBI: The main obstacles and problems in the growth of industrial units are the paucity of primary infrastructure, unavailability of suitable market to selling the products, working capital requirement and difficulties arising out of the delays receiving the bills. Considering these problems, the following provisions are included in the various schemes of SIDBI.

- Loan assistance to the institutions providing market or marketing avenues to the small entrepreneurs.
- Loan assistance to ancillary units and also for modernization and upgrading technology.
- Loan assistance to institutions providing primary services and infrastructure and develop the growth centres.
- Loan assistance to NSIC.
- Loan assistance to institutions providing primary services and infrastructure and developing the growth centres.

Nature of the Loan Assistance Scheme is as follows:

- Refinance to SSIDCs which supply raw material to small units and provide them mark avenues.
- Bill discounting facility.
- Refinance for loan given by state level institutions and banks under the single window system for fixed capital and working capital.
- Refinance of loan given to certified professionals and self-employed people for business like small clinics and hospitals, nursing homes, development of tourism, etc.
- Refinance for loan given by banks and concerned institutions for new projects, expansion and modernization of existing units, quality improvement and rehabilitation of the units.

Appendix

Appendix

Women Entrepreneurship in Andhra Pradesh: A Case Study

This Appendix is devoted to promotion of women entrepreneurship in Ranga Reddy, Krishna and Chittoor districts of Andhra Pradesh.

Development Agencies in Andhra Pradesh

Andhra Pradesh State Financial Corporation: The APSFC is one of the pioneering financial institutions in the state supplying term credit to the medium and small scale industries. It came into existence in 1956. The main functions of APSFC include.

- Sanctioning term loans under IDBI refinancing scheme to industries for purchase and land, building and machinery.
- Guaranteeing purchase of machinery on deferred payments.
- Providing foreign exchange loans under World Bank loan of credit.
- Underwriting of issue of share and debentures.
- Providing seed capital under IDBI seed capital assistance scheme.

Thus APSFC provides financial assistance in the form of term loans, bridge loans, equity participation guaranteeing and underwriting debentures, shares, special capital assistance, to facilitate the growth of small industry. It also sanctions loans/grants to the people intending to establish khadi and village industries. It charges 4 percent rate of interest on loans sanctioned for khadi industries it does not charge any interest. DICs forward applications for sanction of loans and liaise with SFC branches for quick disposal of cases.

Andhra Pradesh State Small Industries Development Corporation: The Andhra Pradesh Industries Development Corporation Ltd. Was established in 1972, by the Government of Andhra Pradesh.

The functions of the corporation are:

- Providing infrastructural facilities;
- Supplying scarce raw materials; and
- Marketing assistance to small units.

The Corporation is basically meant to provide support and sustaining functions and as such it has nothing to do with stimulatory functions. The corporation is not engaged in conducting entrepreneurship development programmes for the promotion of entrepreneurship. The services of the corporation are availed by the existing entrepreneurs.

Andhra Pradesh Industrial Infrastructure Corporation: Development of industrial infrastructure was under the control of the Director of Industries till 1973. In 1973 a separate corporation was established in Andhra Pradesh known as the Andhra Pradesh Industrial Infrastructure Corporation. The strategic functions of the corporation include:

- Acquisition of land and establishment of industrial estates and development areas.
- Construction of sheds and development of plots with infrastructure facilities like internal roads, water supply and power supply.
- Coordination with government organisations to provide transport, post office, telephone and other facilities in the industrial estates.
- Payment of voluntary loan contribution to Andhra Pradesh State Electricity Board on behalf of the entrepreneurs for arranging power supply.

The APIIC has taken up the responsibility of establishing industrial estates for the benefit of small entrepreneurs, wherein ready sheds with all infrastructure facilities will be provided to establish industrial units. Industrial development areas are established to provide developed plots for establishing small, medium and large industries. This corporation, therefore, provides the advantage of relieving the small entrepreneurs from procedural delays and problem, municipal permission, etc. GM, DIC is the Chairman of the Plot/Shed Allotment Committee of APIC at the district level. He is also a member of the APIIC Advisory Committee.

Andhra Pradesh Industrial and Technical Consultancy Organisation: The APITCO was established along with other Technical Consultancy Organisations by the IDBI in 1978. The functions of APITCO are as follows:

- Publicity of entrepreneurial opportunity;
- Entrepreneurial education;
- Motivation or training to prospective entrepreneurs;
- Identification of entrepreneurs;
- Inplant training to entrepreneurs;
- Help and guidance in selecting the product;
- Arranging techno-economic information to entrepreneurs;
- Preparing and evaluating the project;
- Making available the product profile;
- Evolving locally suitable and new product and processes;
- Training personnel for counselling and promotion of entrepreneurship;
- Offering entrepreneurial counselling;
- Organizing entrepreneurial counselling;
- Help and guidance in selecting and obtaining machinery;
- Offering managerial consultancy;
- Helping in marketing of the product;
- Help and guide in expanding the unit; and
- Help and guide in replacement of equipment and processes.

The target group of this organization are the new entrepreneurs of first generation and existing entrepreneurs who are already in business. The organization has gained a rich fund of experience in identification of potential entrepreneurs besides developing a vast and extensive network with institutions and agencies engaged in the development of small and medium scale units. Apart from conducting its own programmes, APITCO is called upon by other institutions/agencies in conducting Entrepreneurship Development Programme, Project appraisal and Training the Trainers.

Small Industries Service Institutes: The Small Industries Assistance Programme when it was launched in 1954 aimed at providing an integrated industrial service for the development of small industries. The three main ingredients of this service were technical management and economic improvements required for developing a modern small industry sector. Besides this, various types of assistance relating to finance, raw materials, worksheds etc., were also provided. However, for ensuring the required impact of these inputs, the small industrial units needed requisite technical and managerial standard. The small scale Industries Development Organisation Programme was, therefore, primarily aimed at providing these services through a network of Small Industries Service Institutes and Extension Centres and to coordinate the assistance programme of the various State Governments and other agencies relating to small industry development.

At a time when the small industry sector was emerging as a distinct factory sector with modern techniques of production and using modern types of machinery and technical processes, technical services among others formed a leading plank of service to modernize the small industry structure. Provision of technical know-how covered not only the existing small nits but also a large number of new small units, so as to utilize the abundant resources in material and skills, otherwise lying untapped for industrial development. This involved development of new technical processes and skills apart from the improvement of existing ones.

Federation of Andhra Pradesh Chamber of Commerce & Industry (Women Wing): FAPCCI was established in

1959 with the support of the Ministry of Commerce, Government of India. Padmashri Late A.R. Bhat evolved this concept of Association creating an apex body and he was instrumental in the very edifice of FAPCCI and forest this great organization for the benefit of Small Industry Movement. FAPCCI has been rendering its services for the small industry in our country. This organization has been established on the lines of FICCI and ASSOCHAM, which have emerged as principle spokesmen for the big business.

The FAPCCI has following objectives:

- To cooperate with industrial, business, educational and research institutes, and other organizations in connection with exchange of information pertaining to small industries;
- To organize common service facilities for its members;
- To cooperate with other small industry associations with the intention of furthering the objectives of the federation;
- To conduct, undertake the conduct of/participate in national and international exhibitions;
- To promote marketing groups and undertake such activities for marketing small industry products; and
- To conduct special type of training programmes, seminars, conferences, conventions and such other meetings to promote the technology and economic status and growth of small scale industries.

Association of Lady Entrepreneurs of Andhra Pradesh: ALEAP was the dream of like minded women entrepreneurs who wanted to train, guide, support and enhance the lives of ladies. The Association of Lady Entrepreneurs of Andhra Pradesh was established with an aim to bring Women Entrepreneurs trying to help each other and work in collaboration for welfare maximization. The Association was established in December 1993 and today holds the recognition of being one of India's premier institutions of women entrepreneurs totally devoted to the development of entrepreneurship among women. It is an organization of enterprising women who have one common-desire to help other women, who want to start it. It is a state level organization with an objective of upliftment of women and empowerment through establishing small and medium enterprises.

ALEAP has built up a strong support network with Government and non-Government organizations, working with them to provide other required facilities for entrepreneurship development. The Association has the credit of conducting various training programmes in India and Sri Lanka in collaboration with different Organisations. The members are mostly first generation entrepreneurs, and they have to their credit outstanding achievements. The mission of the Association is to spearhead entrepreneurial movement throughout the state with a belief that entrepreneurs need not be born but can be developed through well conceived and well directed activities.

The objectives of the Association are:

- Assist women in identifying project, programmes and schemes for upliftment;
- Encourage women entrepreneurs to market their products and compete in the market successfully;
- Organise exhibitions, seminars and vendor development programmes;
- Assist women to learn and acquire entrepreneurial qualities through several programmes.
- Provide infrastructure facilities to the members with an objective to encourage industrial growth;
- Liase between Government and Entrepreneurs by providing necessary information and help women entrepreneurs by providing necessary consultancy; and
- Help entrepreneurs overcome gender-related barriers.

The Association has established the Centre for Entrepreneurship Development, a wholly autonomous body set up in the year 1997, supported by Central and State Government with an aim to transform women into able entrepreneurs. Yet another landmark is the ALEAP Credit, a company incorporated under the Companies Act for implementation of Mutual Credit Guarantee Scheme.

District Industries Centres: The District Industries Centre Programme was launched on 1st May, 1978, to provide a focal point for promotion of small, village and cottage industries and to provide all services and support to the decentralized industrial sector under a single roof at pre-investment, investment and post investment stages.

The scheme lays great emphasis on manning the DICs with personnel of proven ability and adequate experience having quality of leadership, organizational ability and executive capability. Accordingly, the State Governments have been advised that wherever adequate number of suitable persons from their existing agencies and department could not be identified, recruitment may be thrown open to such persons from open market and at the same time efforts should be made to draw persons on deputation basis from other Government departments and organizations.

The functions performed by the DIC are as follows:

- Publicity of entrepreneurial opportunities;
- Entrepreneurial education;
- Identification of entrepreneurs;
- Motivation or training to prospective entrepreneurs;
- Help and guidance in selecting the product;
- Preparing the evaluating the project;
- Arranging techno-economic information to entrepreneurs;
- Offering entrepreneurial counselling;
- Registering the unit;
- Arranging finance on credit;
- Help and guide in selecting and obtaining machinery and equipment;
- Supplying scarce raw material;
- Assisting in quality control;
- Help and guide in expanding the unit; and
- Help and guide in replacement of equipment.

Support and Sustaining Functions of Development Institutions/Agencies

The support and sustaining functions are detailed below.

Support Functions

- Registering the unit;
- Arranging finance on credit;
- Providing shed, power, water etc.;
- Help and guidance in selecting machinery and equipment;
- Supplying scarce raw material;
- Providing common facility centres;
- Assisting in quality control; and
- Offering managerial consultancy.

Sustaining Functions

- Help in marketing of the product;
- Help in modernizing the unit;
- Help and guide in expanding the unit; and
- Help and guide in replacement of equipment.

Land and Power: Granting that all inputs for the development of industries are made available to the small and medium scale sector, most vital problem has been that of electric power shortage. This is a problem which has been confronting the industrialists throughout the country.

Inadequate and untimely supply of power has been one of the major problems faced by the newly established units. Delay in getting power connections for new units in some cases extend up to 2 years causing enormous difficulties to new small and medium sized units. They have to bear the interest burden on idle plant and machinery if already installed. By the time they get power connection and start production cost escalations may throw their production plans out of gear. Existing units also do suffer, peak load restrictions etc., upsetting their production schedules.

50 percent of the Women Entrepreneurs from various forms of organizations in Ranga Reddy district, 68.33 percent in Krishna district and 40 percent in Chittoor district were of the opinion that the District industries centre helped there in

getting land and electricity supply for their units, while the remaining Women Entrepreneurs felt that the district industries centres did not help them in procuring the same for their industrial units. The same view has been echoed by Women Entrepreneurs with different educational background and varying age groups of Women Entrepreneurs.

Role of Institutions in Providing Financial Assistance: Small Scale units usually suffer on account of bad debts as a result of which the entrepreneur will be losing money. Small scale units and ancillary units supply finished goods or components to Government department, large industries etc. The goods or components are sold on credit and the payment is made any time between 3 months. As a result of which the funds blocked in these credit sales and the small scale unit finds itself in a position whereby it is unable to carry on its operations for want of funds.

Decisions on capital structure are unfortunately influenced by the extent to which loans are available. It is a pity that the real consideration which should be taken into account in deciding the debt capacity, such as profitability, the scope for growth etc., are not considered at all. The result is that by the time units pose through the construction stage and when production commences, the earnings are inadequate for payments of interest. The result is that a number of small scale units are never allowed to reach a stage of profitable operations in spite of the fact that the units may be in a viable industry and the economics of its production and sales may be quite sound.

When considering the quantum of long term funds required for a unit, sufficient attention is normally not paid to the amount of the working capital required to be provided from long term funds. Working capital is not an immediate problem for a unit at the stage of erection of plant and machinery. Because of the escalations in the total cost of the project which again is usually not taken into consideration in estimating the total investment, the entire long term funds would have been used up by the time the project is complete. From the first day of its operations, it has to depend upon short term sources of working capital. Depletion of resources also takes place in a small scale unit whereby the capital, deposits and resources are completely eroded when the concern incur losses continuously. When the creditors come to know about this, they will exert pressure on the unit to make payments immediately whereby the problem gets intensified.

The small scale units may not get any financial assistance from banks as the reserves and capital have eroded. Owners or partners of small scale units resort to the withdrawal of funds for meeting their personal obligations or for investing elsewhere. As a result of such withdrawals or diversion of funds, the small scale units do not have the necessary funds to carry on its business activity. Withdrawals/diversion of funds are more prevalent in small scale units because there is no control over the owners/partners/directors etc. The main source of growth for small businesses is through retention of earnings. This is the buffer against which borrowings can be made. A small business has to grow from within by the retention of earnings. Withdrawals represent a drain. Sacrifices in this area have to be made by the owners, at least in the early part of the life of the business.

The financial factors creating sick small units take the form of defective financing of fixed and working capital. The defective financing of working capital has more serious effect that the defective financing of fixed capital on the working of the production units rendering them sick small units. The defective financing may take the form of under financing, delayed financing and high cost of financing. The under financing of working capital for the production units is said to be done when a banker provides inadequate working capital to the units making them reap huge losses. Under financing of working capital may also be attributed to the defective estimation of the need based working capital for the production units.

Under financing of working capital is not conducive to the healthy working of the units as it results in working below capacity, high cost of production and the incapability on the part of the small scale units to reap the economics. The high cost of financing working capital will push up the production cost which is not conducive to the healthy working of the units when they are just able to meet average variable costs and part of the fixed costs. The increased production costs over the revenue yields will result in huge losses.

50 percent of the Women Entrepreneurs from various forms of organisation in Ranga Reddy District followed by 68.33 percent in Krishna district and 40 percent in Chittoor district were of the opinion that the district industries centres helped their in obtaining financial assistance for their units while the remaining Women Entrepreneurs said they did not receive any help in securing financial assistance through the District Industries Centres. The same opinion prevails among the Women Entrepreneurs with different educational back ground and different age groups.

Role of Banks: Commercial banks have an important role to play in the flow of institutional finance particularly in a country like India. Even though a number of financial institutions have been set up both at the national and state level, the commercial banks have to supplement the efforts by ensuring flow of funds in the priority sectors such as agriculture, industry etc.

The commercial banks till nationalization have been eager to assist the large industry and thereby the small scale sector was given a raw deal. The origin of small industry financing can be traced to 1956. The State Bank of India has been in the forefront of development banking activity in the country, took up the challenge of financing small scale industries in 1956. A pilot scheme of financing small scale industries was introduced on the April 1, 1956. During the year twenty five small scale units were financed with an aggregate of about Rs. 1 million spread over nine collected branches. Satisfied with the pilot scheme, the Bank launched its liberalized scheme of assistance to small scale industries at all its branches. The scheme was so named as it introduced certain liberalizations over the existing terms and conditions under which bank finance was hitherto extended to industry, which was mostly restricted to the large sector.

Financing of small scale industries called for a radical reappraisal of the various accepted standards and methods of lending. A complete departure from the conventional approach has been made in appraising loan applications and advances are being sanctioned as a need-based performance oriented approach.

The Women Entrepreneurs from various forms of organisation in Krishna district appear to be satisfied about the role of the district industries centre in obtaining bank assistance since 68.33 percent have responded favourably while 50 percent the Women Entrepreneurs in Ranga Reddy district and 40 percent in Chittoor district have been beneficiaries of the bank assistance. The Women Entrepreneurs with different educational background and age group, three districts are also of the same view.

Raw Materials: It is necessary that a policy decision be taken at a highest level that a certain percentage of any indigenous raw materials be reserved for the small scale sector. Such a reservation could be done best on the basis of past consumption of the raw materials coupled with the projected requirements, depending on the growth rate. This would ensure that the small scale units get the same proportion of their requirements in scarcity condition as well. The policy adopted by the canalizing agencies to distribute imported material on first come first served basis, obviously works to the advantage of large units. Moreover a specific responsibility should be cast on the canalizing agencies to see that a fixed proportion of the total available material goes to the small scale units. The Government of Andhra Pradesh lose no time in ensuring that imported raw materials are distributed to the small scale sector precisely on the same basis as those for large units and that a fair proportion of the indigenous production should be allocated to the small scale sector.

In order to meet the criticism of the indigenous producers and the canalizing agencies that the demand put forward by the small scale sector are inflated, it is necessary to make a precise assessment of the future requirements of the small scale sector from time to time. Such as assessment can be done by a Tripartite Committee at the State Level consisting of Director of Industries, Andhra Pradesh Small Industries Development Corporation and the State Associations. It should be done on the basis of norms set up by Development Commissioner for a particular item or group of items. It should then be possible on the basis of units registered with Director of Industries to make a realistic assessment of the need of any specific commodity for the units in the state. This exercise has become very necessary not only to project the realistic figures but also for a long term planning in regard to the quantum of materials which we have to import for the coming years.

The Small Industries Development Corporation which is primarily created to work as 'Raw Material Bank' for the small scale sector should be entrusted to take up such a function without further delay. This is more due to the fact that the District Industries Programme which has been launched would need much more flexibility at the State level, so far as the distribution of raw material is concerned. The Central canalizing agencies cannot be expected to have the special consideration for the tiny and very small units to be located in the rural sector.

68.33 percent of the Women Entrepreneurs from various forms of organisation in Krishna district followed by 50 percent of the Women Entrepreneurs in Ranga Reddy district and 40 percent of the Women Entrepreneurs in Chittoor district have lauded the role of the District Industries Centres in the procurement of raw materials while the remaining Women Entrepreneurs did not subscribe to their views. The same views were upheld by Women Entrepreneurs hailing from different age groups and educational back ground.

Marketing: Marketing is considered to be a very important function by manufacturing units irrespective of the fact whether it is small, medium or large. Marketing is the performance of business activities that directs the flow of goods and services from producer to consumer or user. Industrial production is mostly done in anticipation of the future demand and hence manufacturing units will have to devise ways and means of selling the products to the customers. Manufacturers are compelled to put in their maximum efforts in order to sell their products to the ultimate consumers in the face of stiff competition. Small scale units are always at a disadvantage when compared to the medium of large scale units as they do not have extensive marketing organization and at the same time they are not able to bring the products to the notice of the customers due to lack of publicity.

Though the responsibility for better and improved methods of distribution of small industry products are that of the small scale units, but still the state has been following a deliberate policy of ensuring small industry development and promotion as part of its national objectives of widening employment opportunities. Small scale units usually look to the state for more help in regard to the marketing and distribution of small industry products.

The Central Government stores purchase programme is one of the most important programmes which provide an outlet for the products of the industrial units in the country. The programme is being operated by the Director General of Supplies and Disposals, Government of India. Under this programme, DGS&D is responsible for arranging purchase and delivery of all stores required by the Central Government.

68.33 percent of the Women Entrepreneurs from various forms of organisations in Krishna district, 50 percent in Ranga Reddy district, and 40 percent of the Women Entrepreneurs in Chittoor district said that they received assistance from the respective District Industries Centre in marketing of their products while the remaining Women Entrepreneurs were of the view that necessary assistance was not forth coming in marketing their products. Women entrepreneurs with different educational background and age groups seem to have similar view with regard to the role of District Industries Centres in marketing their products.

Exports: Export plays an important role for boosting the tempo of economic development. In the context of developing economy, the technique of export promotional aspects has to be given due attention. The surplus balance of payment and economic stability can be achievable by generating export promotional aspects. The strategy of export planning for India is an important issue which needs greater attention and rigorous direction in administration. Export trade is not as simple as selling in the domestic market. In International Trade, the exporter has to send his goods abroad and thus get involved in the complex procedures and formalities relating to transport of goods, customs authorities and foreign exchange regulating authorities. These long arduous procedures and formalities make foreign trade complicated and cumbersome. This is one of the reasons as to why a number of small scale units have not paid much attention to this outlet.

There is also an imperative need to vitalize the small scale industrial sector for producing the qualitative type of commodities which can command stability at the international competitive market. Such a line of direction, does assure great importance, as small scale industries do play as important role for generating the export promotional prospects.

50 percent of the Women Entrepreneurs from various forms of organisation in Ranga Reddy district, followed by 68.33 percent of the Women Entrepreneurs in Krishna district and 40 percent of the Women entrepreneurs in Chittoor district acknowledged the assistance of the district industries centres in export of their products. Women entrepreneurs from different educational background and different age groups in the three

districts also held the same view.

Management Consultancy Services: The most important cause for industrial sickness is due to lack of managerial competence. The successful running of small scale units is based on efficient and sound management. It is the managerial competence which makes the difference between successful small units and unsuccessful small units keeping the availability of resources constant. While some optimism is a virtue, excessive optimism can spell disaster. Small Women Entrepreneurs are often so optimistic that they fail to recognize and deal with problem promptly.

Lack of managerial competence may be because of the poor managerial talent in the newly established small and medium scale units. These units are usually manned by persons who are financially strong or technically competent. But these persons do not have the qualities which are expected to run their units successfully. As a result of which the financial soundness or the technical expertise cannot be made effective use. These persons usually lack traits such as supervisory ability, initiative, creative thinking, maturity in decision making etc. as a result of which the management is inefficient.

71.67 percent of the Women Entrepreneurs from various forms of organisation in Ranga Reddy district were dissatisfied or less satisfied about the consultancy services while 76.67 percent of the Women Entrepreneurs in Chittoor district and 46.67 percent in Krishna District were of the same view. Women Entrepreneurs with different educational background and age groups in Ranga Reddy district is 50 percent, 68.33 percent in Krishna district, and 40 percent in Chittoor district held similar opinion about the management consultancy service offered by the District Industries Centres.

Extension Services: 68.33 percent of the Women Entrepreneurs from various forms of organization and Educational Background in Krishna district, 50 percent in Ranga Reddy district, and 40 percent in Chittoor district were of favourable opinion about the extension services offered by the DICS and the remaining were unfavourable.

Only 18.33 percent of the Women Entrepreneurs from different age groups in Ranga Reddy district, 13.33 percent in Chittoor district and 31.67 percent in Krishna district were satisfied about the quality of extension of services while the remaining Women Entrepreneurs were either less satisfied or dissatisfied.

Contact with Other Co-Participants: Only 68.33 percent of the Women Entrepreneurs from different forms of organization, Educational Background and Age groups in Krishna district, 50 percent in Ranga Reddy district and 40 percent in Chittoor district were satisfied with the contact with other co-participants of the programme, while the remaining women entrepreneurs were either less satisfied or dissatisfied.

Prerequisites of Successful Entrepreneurship

The need to identify Women Entrepreneurs has in turn led to speculation both plain and scientific, regarding the characteristics of potential entrepreneurs. The results of this are a spate of hypothetical models regarding entrepreneurial characteristics and 'entrepreneurial syndrome'. The term 'entrepreneurial syndrome' refers to a cluster of characteristics social, economic and behavioural, which are found to consistently occur in a pattern in different manners among successful and unsuccessful entrepreneurs. In most developing countries, there has been a realization of the role of small enterprises in overall economic development and consequently, efforts are afoot to device ways and means of analyzing, identifying nurturing and promoting entrepreneurial behaviour. It needs no emphasis that while governments may provide finance, technical guidance, raw material and other resources, it is ultimately only a set of enterprising individuals who can make the best use of these facilities.

In the final analysis, the role of the characteristics associated with the success of entrepreneurship personal, social and psychological, individually or in combination, stands out significantly. And it appears possible and perhaps necessary to develop ways and means of identifying potential Women Entrepreneurs who could be encouraged and supported on a selective basis. It is not suggested that one could arrive at a universally applicable and invariant portrait of an entrepreneur. But what is advocated is the view that in every society some people possess entrepreneurial qualities to a greater degree than other, and these people have to be involved to take advantage of development activity. While entrepreneurial behaviour can be readily identified as a common pattern, the underlying roots of such behaviour seems to vary from culture to culture.

In order to identify the prerequisites of successful entrepreneurship, the 180 respondents belonging to three districts were asked to rank them in order of importance. Accordingly, the respondents ranked the prerequisites in the following order.

- Commitment to work
- High Quality Product
- Good Marketing Strategy
- Adequate Expert Knowledge
- Adequate Resources
- One's inborn capability
- Time Management
- Ability to Perceive
- Future Planning
- Fate or Chance Factors

The Mean rank order shows that on an average, women Entrepreneurs regarded "Commitment to work" as the primary prerequisite of successful entrepreneurs. In other words, on an average, dedicated and since work is given utmost importance in order to ensure success in entrepreneurial ventures.

The second factor of importance has been found to be high quality products. This implies that on an average, women entrepreneurs consider quality of the product to be very essential factor for success in entrepreneurship, although, it is not felt to be as important as commitment to work. This factor is followed by 'Good Marketing Strategy', which is indicative of the fact that women entrepreneurs are fully conscious of the necessities of technical and professional skills of marketing in entrepreneurship.

The fourth factor in order of importance has been observed to be 'Adequate Expert Knowledge'. The respondents consider expertise and professionalism to be quite essential for success in business ventures. The next factor in order of importance is 'Adequate Resources' in the form of money, personnel, technology, materials, professional advice followed by 'one's inborn capability'.

'Time Management' has been observed to be given the next rank, which implies that although this is considered an important factor, but not as essential as the other factors mentioned above. The respondents have given the rank to the factor 'ability to perceive' and to the factor 'future planning'; the factor of 'fate and chance' has received the least rank in order of importance as compared to the other nine factors. This implies that women entrepreneurs do not attach much importance to external factors as influencing success in entrepreneurship. On the contrary, work commitment, good quality of product and marketing strategies are ranked as more important.

Entrepreneurial Characteristics

Risk-taking propensity can be divided into Personal risk-taking and delegation of authority and responsibility component of risk taking. Accordingly, it can be observed that women entrepreneurs rate in personal risk-taking is high i.e., taking risks in their personal lives, while with regard to delegation of authority, women entrepreneurs take moderate risks in the form of delegation of authority to staff and subordinates. With regard to independence orientation, it is found that on an average, women entrepreneurs are very independent. They prefer autonomy of thought and action and believe in self-sufficiency.

Need for achievement falls in the high category of scores, which goes to prove that women entrepreneurs in India are achievement oriented.

As regards the decision making ability, women entrepreneurs make quick decisions, prefer to decide independently, learn from mistakes made in previous decisions and try to overcome difficult problems actively instead of avoiding them.

Women entrepreneurs have a high score on decision making ability, implying that they make quick decisions, prefer to decide independently, learn from mistakes and try to overcome difficult problems.

It can be inferred that women entrepreneurs quite frequently engage in planning for business growth, expansion and diversification while with regard to Time Management, women entrepreneurs manage their time efficiently only on an average degree and there is still a lot to manage time more effectively.

Personal Risk Taking in Select Districts

As regards the Personal risk taking ability of women entrepreneurs in the select districts, it is observed that the women entrepreneurs of Ranga Reddy have exhibited risk taking ability in four of the five characteristics. In the case of Women entrepreneurs of Krishna District also, the same trend is evident but only next to the women entrepreneurs in Ranga Reddy District. The women entrepreneurs of Chittoor District have also demonstrated the same characteristics, but on a lesser scale when compared to the other districts. As the entrepreneurial function primarily involves risk measurement and risk taking it is imperative that women entrepreneurs should be willing to take personal risks thus enabling them to take business risks.

Independence Orientation

The second entrepreneurial characteristic is independence orientation which is measured by seven items and these are given for three districts.

Women entrepreneurs from Ranga Reddy, Krishna and Chittoor Districts mostly made decisions on their own, while a good number made independent decisions. The women entrepreneurs in the sample reported that they disliked interference from others. A majority of the respondents stated they always liked taking initiative. All the women entrepreneurs reported that they strived for self-sufficiency, while a good number of respondents liked having freedom of action. Women entrepreneurs disliked people who forced their opinion on them.

Thus, it can be inferred that self-sufficiency and independence are the important characteristics of women entrepreneurs in the three districts of Andhra Pradesh.

Need for Achievement

The third entrepreneurial characteristic is need for achievement which is measured by 10 items for the women entrepreneurs in the three districts.

Need for achievement is one the most widely researched entrepreneurial characteristic. It is also referred to as the urge to improve by McClelland. High achievement oriented individuals have been found to take personal responsibility for their actions, to persist in the face of obstacles and to do things creatively.

The results are indicative of moderately high achievement orientation among women entrepreneurs in the three select districts. Majority of the women entrepreneurs always concentrated on higher goals and do not consider work very hard. The respondents reported that in spite of obstacles and hindrances they could do their work very well.

50 percent of the sample women entrepreneurs in all the three districts reported that they always wanted to maintain a

high level of performance. Majority of the women entrepreneurs in the three districts were always prepared to meet emergency situation on the job, while moderate took pleasure in performing new and challenging tasks.

The results depict that women entrepreneurs always prefer difficult goals which require more effort in achieving them, and a majority always believed in goal setting and its attainment. As regards competition, the sample women entrepreneurs always liked competition. It appears that achievement orientation is moderately high among women entrepreneurs.

Decision-Making

The fourth entrepreneurial characteristic is decision-making and is measured by 10 items with regard to the sample women entrepreneurs in the three districts. The results clearly indicate that women entrepreneurs have high decision making ability. A majority of the women entrepreneurs in the three districts have been observed to respond positively to all the 10 items. Majority of the women entrepreneurs feel that one should make quick decisions, have creative solutions for problems, learn from mistakes made in previous decisions and not to delay in making decisions.

It is observed that a sizeable number of women entrepreneurs had missed opportunities because they waited too long to decide.

Future Planning

An overwhelming majority of women entrepreneurs felt that it was always necessary to plan for the future, to set long term targets, to plan business strategies by using growth and expansion opportunities and to have new outlets as a business strategy. As far as a change in product was concerned, the women entrepreneurs felt that only sometimes, changes in products was desirable. From these results, it is amply evident that women entrepreneurs consider future planning to be an invaluable strategy for business growth and expansion.

Time Management

Time management is the sixth entrepreneurial characteristic and is measured by 10 items for the women entrepreneurs in Ranga Reddy, Krishna and Chittoor Districts of Andhra Pradesh.

Time is the most precious, yet the most limited resource for entrepreneurs. It is observed that majority of the respondents identify specific goals for themselves as a time management strategy; establish deadlines, use telephone, fax, internet instead of personal visit. Majority of the women entrepreneurs reported that they use every minute productively, while only a small number question their use of time. On the whole, it appears that punctuality for appointments and being ready for each days work are the most commonly adopted techniques for time management, while questioning one's use of time and doing only essential duties are the least used and popular techniques.

It is heartening to note that the institutions/agencies which have been discussed, have been instrumental in the promotion of women entrepreneurship. Some of these institutions have been established by the Central Government and some by the Government of A.P. It would be unreasonable to expect these state sponsored institutions alone to play a positive role in the development of women entrepreneurship. The Women Organisations and Voluntary Non Governmental Organisations should also come forward, and extend a helping hand to the state sponsored institutions in promoting the women entrepreneur ship in A.P. It is worth mentioning that institutions/agencies such as Federation of Andhra Pradesh Chambers of Commerce & Industry, Association of Lady women entrepreneurs of Andhra Pradesh, Federation of Indian Women entrepreneurs have been playing a complementary role in A.P. Thus, there is a need for more voluntary organizations to come forward and cooperate with other institutions in this national task of training the women entrepreneurs. Hence, the hypothesis that 'Voluntary Non-Governmental Organisations also play an active role in the promotion of women entrepreneurship on par with the state sponsored institutions' is accepted.

From the mapping of organizational functions of these institutions for A.P. and Ranga Reddy, Krishna & Chittoor Districts, it is abundantly clear that most of these institutions consider the stimulatory functions alone as the most important task, thus relegating the support and sustaining functions to the background. Thus, we find that there is a lopsided development in these institutions, wherein stimulatory functions are given top priority, while the support and sustaining functions are given least importance. Considering the fact that the incidence of sickness in the small enterprises is high, these institutions should also strive to undertake support and sustaining functions which alone, will infuse the much needed confidence amongst the women entrepreneurs.
Hence, the hypothesis that 'the whole efforts to promote and develop entrepreneurship of three groups of functions viz., stimulatory, support and sustenance. All these occur in a cycle and play a complementary role to each other. The institutions/agencies balance all the three functions' is rejected.

Motivational Climate of Institutions/Agencies

The motivational climate of an organization refers to the major concern of the personnel in the organization. The personnel may hate to perform many activities in the task of promoting entrepreneurship. The manner in which the personnel perform their task is largely dependent on the motivational concern. The motivational concern among the personnel in this task, leads to the building of a proper climate for the institutions/agencies. The motivational concerns can be broadly grouped into five categories: (i) Achievement; (ii) Affiliation; (iii) Dependence; (iv) Extension; and (v) Power.

The achievement concern refers to doing a task better to

achieve a standard of excellence, accomplishing something unique, innovative, creative and important. The personnel in an organization having 'achievement' as a dominant concern will not hesitate to undertake certain risks to achieve something new, unique, or challenging, so that they are different from other organizations.

The affiliation concern seeks warm, friendly, compassionate relationships. An organization having affiliation as dominant concern usually foregoes all types of achievement for the sake of harmonious relations among the personnel. The personnel in those organizations lack the initiative and are not adventurous. They derive satisfaction in maintaining status quo.

The Dependency concern represents the performance of routine tasks and compliance of orders from above. An organization having dependency as a major concern usually lack initiative and adhere to rules and regulations from above for all their actions.

The extension concern describes an urge to benefit other by extending appropriate help and guidance, taking up challenging tasks and/or influencing or directing the behaviour of others. An organization having dominant extension concern, designs and attempts many new and suitable programmes and strategies to benefit others.

The power concern signifies the exercise of influence and control in order to change other's behaviour or to gain a position of authority and status. The members of an organization with power as dominant concern derive satisfaction by controlling and influencing the behaviour of others.

The organization climate as perceived by the women entrepreneurs is that the APITCO is predominantly "extension achievement" oriented. Such a climate is most conducive for carrying out a development task like entrepreneurship development. Many a time the personnel of APITCO have been very innovative in finding ways and means to help and guide women entrepreneurs so that they may succeed in setting and running their units. This is because of the achievement concern. Since the concern is dominant, they want to attain a certain standard of excellence in performance the task of women entrepreneurship development.

In the case of SISI and APSFC the most dominant concern has been 'Extension". Greater extension concern among officers of these organisations indicates an urge to help others by extending appropriate help and guidance taking up innovative work and adopting new strategies with the ultimate objective to benefit others. The two organizations also have two different supportive concerns- 'affiliation' for SISI and 'achievement' for APSFC. The SISI, thus has an 'Extension Affiliation' dominated climate. This suggests that along with due concern to benefit clients, the personnel are also concerned about friendly relations among themselves. Assumption of responsibility is seldom done and at the same time delegation of power to share work is rather minimal. The personnel, although exhibiting concern for their clients, do not like to take the risk of decision-making. The APSFC has extension achievement dominated climate. This shows that the personnel are mostly concerned with providing benefits to women entrepreneurs by achieving certain standard of excellence.

Dependency is the predominant motivational concern in the District Industries Centres at Ranga Reddy, Krishna and Chittoor. Under such a climate there is a general lack of initiative and people display greater adherence to rules and regulations. They seek directive from above for every action. They depend on their superior for every simple action. The DICs have a 'Dependency Power' dominated climate which means that for the personnel the task is important only as a means to obey directives from superiors. The superiors are also bothered only about the achievement of physical target. The quality of the output hardly matters. Due to power dominance, the decision-making is more of a status symbol and operational and functional desirability is only secondary or incidental. This sort of climate does not enable the personnel engaged in the task of entrepreneurship development to take quick and prompt decisions.

Clientele Satisfaction of Stimulatory Functions

The level of satisfaction expressed by the 180 sample women entrepreneurs with respect to the activities of the various promotional institutions/agencies was measured through a clientele satisfaction scale.

Eight institutions/agencies in various functions were evaluated and the clientele satisfaction was measured. The Andhra Pradesh State Financial Corporation, Andhra Pradesh State Small Industries Development Corporation, Andhra Pradesh Industrial Infrastructure Corporation, Andhra Pradesh Industrial & Technical Consultancy Organisation, Association of Lady women entrepreneurs of A.P. have been rated as High in the clientele satisfaction by the sample women entrepreneurs. In the case of Small Industries Service Institute and the Federation of Andhra Pradesh Chambers of Commerce & Industry (Women's Wing) have been rated as Medium in the clientele satisfaction. The highlight is that no institutions/agency has been ranked as 'Low' in the clientele satisfaction.

The institutions/agencies covered in the present study, are very effectively performing the stimulatory functions in the promotion of women entrepreneurship and hence the reason for ranking these institution as 'High' and 'Medium' in the clientele satisfaction. The basic objective in developing women entrepreneurship and multiplying them in the society has been to enable the society generate productive human resources, mobilize and sustain the same in subsequent process of development. The spontaneity and continuity of the process would depend on the kind of women that can be promoted and groomed in the entrepreneurial career. It is in this context, that institutions discussed in the foregoing paragraphs can play the role of a catalyst in transforming the human potential into a valuable national resource.

Clientele Satisfaction of Support and Sustaining Functions

The level of satisfaction, as expressed by the sample women entrepreneurs has been computed by following the procedure as stated in the preceding paragraphs. As stated earlier, the respondents have expressed their level of satisfaction with regard to institutions/agencies engaged in the promotion of women entrepreneurs about stimulatory functions. The institutions/agencies have been categorized into 'High' and 'Medium', whereas no institution has been rated as 'Low', which implies that the role played by these institutions/ agencies in stimulating the women entrepreneurs, has been widely commended.

In Table 7.33, the level of satisfaction of the respondents have been computed, to rank them as 'High', 'Medium' and 'Low', and accordingly, it is observed that all the eight institutions which are rendering support functions, have been ranked as 'Low' by the women entrepreneurs. It is unfortunate that institutions, which have been ranked as 'High' and 'Medium' in stimulatory functions, have been categorized as 'Low' by the women entrepreneurs, which leads us to the conclusion, that these institutions have a strong base in stimulatory functions and are weak with regard to the support functions. Thus, there is no balance is performing the functions by these institutions. It would be pertinent to point out that, stimulatory functions however effectively performed by these institutions, alone will not create successful women entrepreneurs, provided they are backed by extensive support from these institutions such as arranging finance on credit, providing sheds, power, water, guidance in procuring machinery, arranging supply of scarce raw material, providing common facility centre, quality control and offering managerial consultancy services.

It is time, that these institutions/agencies also evince equal attention to the support functions, to ensure that the dropouts are minimized. It is a common knowledge that ambitious and enterprising women, after undergoing the entrepreneurship development programmes develop high hopes, but when it comes to the implementation of the project, they are confronted with enormous difficulties with regard to the raising of finance, procurement of raw materials, arranging sheds with the necessary infrastructure and getting managerial consultancy services. When these services are not forthcoming, from the institutions/agencies, these enterprising women entrepreneurs abandon their plans to start their units, and finally end up as frustrated dropouts. It is this context that institutions/agencies have to provide the necessary back up and support, to the women entrepreneurs for translating their ideas into implementation.

As regards the clientele satisfaction of sustaining functions of the institutions/agencies, and it is observed that in this case also, the women entrepreneurs of the existing units have ranked all the institutions as 'Low', which is similar to the ranking of the institutions with regard to support functions. Thus, the institutions/agencies are considered to be weak in performing the support and sustaining functions, which will be detrimental to the interests of the women entrepreneurs. Lack of inadequate support and sustaining systems amongst the institutions/agencies, will only lead to the establishment of units which are not viable and unable to compete with the existing units, which can make a vital contribution to accelerating industrial production and generation of employment opportunities. If for nothing else, this dimension of women entrepreneurship development, i.e., providing effective support and sustaining services, deserves more attention and consideration than it has received in the past, in order to ensure that this scourge of industrial sickness does not take its toll in the form of economic as well as social hardships.

The ever growing number of sick enterprises is itself an indication, that there is a dire need to provide support and sustaining functions effectively to the women entrepreneurs, to avoid the colossal waste of human, financial and material resources.

Entrepreneurial Attitude Orientation

Every attitude has an object, be it a specific person, place, thing, event, activity, mental concept, cognitive orientation, life style, or even combinations of the various categories. Attitude also exists at the general and the specific levels for many objects. Because of this, attitude specificity needs to be matched by measurement. Human beings are believed to have stable set of attitudes. However, attitude differs across individuals. Attitudes are not a permanent feature. Attitude towards achievement in general (General Object) is not the same as attitude toward achievement in an entrepreneurial setting (specific object). Personality theory emphasizing personal dispositions of traits and the use of demographic information such as age, sex and birth order are widely used in the studies on entrepreneur ship. Available alternative to personality and demographic approaches is the use of attitudes in predicting behavioural tendencies.

Many research endeavours on EAO are in use since 1990's. Attitudinal approach has been considered to be one of the better alternatives to the study of entrepreneurial personality. Attitudes are assumed to be the prediction of human behaviour. In the current socio psychological context, attitude is defined as pre-disposition to respond in a generally favourable or unfavourable manner with respect to the object of the attitude.

Attitude instrument tend to account to more of the variance in a particular set of behaviour. One of the methodological advantages of the attitude model over the personality model is that it can be more domains specific, thereby reducing unexplained variability and increasing the correlations with behaviour. Retraining and entrepreneurship development are highly positively relate. The four dimensions of EAOS are

- Achievement
- Innovation
- Personal control
- Self-esteem

Achievement: The dimension refers to goal attainment and the action of individual accomplishment of something. Achievement motivation also varies from person to person and it is essential character of an entrepreneur.

Innovation: This dimension refers to sensing and acting upon business dealings in new and peculiar ways. Innovation is an act of starting something for first time, introduce something new. All innovations involve change, but not all changes necessarily involve new ideas or lead to significant improvement.

Personal Control: This dimension refers to the individual perception of control and authority over his or her business. Personal control means, the activity of managing or exerting control over something. It is the degree to which people believe that they are masters of their own fate. Thus the individuals perceived control over the environment were required to influence to one's behaviour.

Self Esteem: People differ in the degree to which they like or dislike themselves. This trait is called self-esteem. Perceived self esteem in business refers to the self confident and personal competency of an individual in connection with business affairs. Self-esteem is directly related to expectations for success high self esteem believe that they posses more of the ability they need in order to succeed at work. Individual with high self esteem will take more risks in job selection and are more likely to choose unconventional jobs than people with low self-esteem. Self esteem is an important personal factor that determines how manager perceive themselves and their role in the organizations.

Findings Regarding Stimulatory Functions

1. As regards the emphasis on Women Entrepreneurship

Development, majority of the women entrepreneurs from Ranga Reddy and Chittoor districts were of the view that the institutions/agencies were only occasionally paying attention to this aspect, while majority of the women entrepreneurs opined that the institutions was placing complete and partial emphasis. Thus, the institutions/agencies have not paid considerable attention in Ranga Reddy and Chittoor Districts, while in the case of Krishna District it is quite contrary.

2. About the promotion of small enterprises by women entrepreneurs in Ranga Reddy, 50 percent stated that the institutions were not paying complete attention, while in Chittoor District the situation is in no way better. The position appears to be much better in Krishna District.
3. The women entrepreneurs from Ranga Reddy District were divided in expressing their opinion about the personnel engaged in training.50 percent termed them as Good, while the remaining stated that they were either less satisfactory or satisfactory. But in the case of Chittoor District, 60 percent of the women entrepreneurs stated that the personnel were good and in Krishna District, the opinion was on similar lines.
4. 50 percent & 40 percent of the women entrepreneurs from Ranga Reddy & Chittoor District felt there was lack of co-operation or Minimum co-operation among the institutions/agencies engaged in promotion of women entrepreneurship. But in the case of Krishna District, nearly 66.67 percent of the women entrepreneurs felt there was perfect co-operation among the institutions and thus had a profound impact on the development of women entrepreneurship in the district.
5. Regarding the effectiveness of Programmes and Courses offered by these Institutions/ Agencies, 50 percent of the entrepreneurs felt that they were effective while 30 percent and 20 percent were of the opinion that they were less effective and ineffective. The same trend appears to

prevail among the women entrepreneurs in Chittoor District. The women entrepreneurs appear to be quite happy with the courses as 68.33 percent stated that they were effective.

6. The methodology adopted in training the women entrepreneurs have come in for sharp criticism, considering the fact that that nearly 50 percent of the women entrepreneurs in Ranga Reddy have stated that they are less satisfactory or satisfactory. Similar is the case with the Chittoor District where 60 percent have termed the methodology as less satisfactory or satisfactory. Only in the case of Krishna District, nearly 68.33 percent have termed the methodology as good, while the remained stated that they were less satisfactory or satisfactory.
7. 50 percent of the women entrepreneurs in Ranga Reddy District have stated that the role of institutions in promoting women entrepreneurship is good, while the remaining termed it as less satisfactory or satisfactory. In the case of Chittoor District, almost 60 percent stated that it was less satisfactory or satisfactory, while the remaining 40 percent felt that the institutions were playing a proactive role in the promotion of women entrepreneurship. In the case of Krishna District, an overwhelming majority of the entrepreneurs were of the opinion that it was good.
8. 68.33 percent of the women entrepreneurs in Krishna District, followed by 50 percent in Ranga Reddy District and 40 percent in Chittoor District stated that they were motivated in starting their enterprises, while the remaining felt on the contrary.
9. In the case of the identification of Potential Women Entrepreneurs also, the same trend can be noticed. 68.33 percent of the women entrepreneurs in Krishna District felt that identification of potential entrepreneurs was done systematically. In the case of Ranga Reddy District, 50 percent felt the same while in the case of Chittoor District

40 percent of the entrepreneurs echoed the same opinion.

10. Regarding the selection of Women Entrepreneurs, 50 percent of the respondents in Ranga Reddy felt that the selection was proper, while the other 50 percent stated that there was lack of proper selection. 40 percent in Chittoor District were of the view that there was proper selection while in Krishna District, 68.33 percent of the women entrepreneurs expressed the same opinion.
11. Regarding the Guidance of Women Entrepreneurs, 50 percent of the respondents in Ranga Reddy District stated that it was good, while 40 percent had the same opinion in Chittoor District. In Krishna District, 68.33 percent felt that the guidance provided to the women entrepreneurs was good.
12. Majority of the respondents in Ranga Reddy District were not happy about the skills possessed by trainers to impart training to the women entrepreneurs. The same trend is visible in Chittoor District. Only in the case of Krishna District, 68.33 percent of the women entrepreneurs stated that the adequacy of skills to impart training was good.
13. 68.33 percent of the women entrepreneurs in Krishna District stated that they received help in the preparation of the Feasibility Report for their enterprises, while it was 50 percent in Ranga Reddy District and 40 percent for Chittoor District.
14. Regarding the post-training contact of institutions by the women entrepreneurs, majority of the respondents in Krishna District maintained contact, while only 50 percent had contact with the institutions in Ranga Reddy District and it was 40 percent in the case of Chittoor District.
15. It can be inferred that women entrepreneurs from Krishna District have been greatly benefited from the stimulatory activities undertaken by the Institutions/Agencies undertaken by the Institutions/Agencies followed by women entrepreneurs in Ranga Reddy District. The women entrepreneurs from Chittoor District have lagged

behind their counterparts in other districts.

Findings Regarding Support and Sustaining Functions

1. 68.33 percent of the respondents in Krishna District, followed by 50 percent in Ranga Reddy and 40 percent stated that they received help from the institutions/agencies in getting land and electricity supply for starting their enterprises.
2. In the case of getting Financial Assistance, the same situation prevails in the case of the women entrepreneurs in the three districts.
3. With regard to Bank Finance for working capital requirements, the women entrepreneurs in Krishna District are fortunate in getting timely assistance, followed by the women entrepreneurs in Ranga Reddy District. The situation appears to be gloomy in the case of Chittoor District.
4. About obtaining of Raw Materials from the canalizing agencies, 68.33 percent of the respondents in Krishna District reported that they got without any difficulty, while 50 percent of the respondents in Ranga Reddy echoed the same view. In Chittoor District, the women entrepreneurs seem to be facing hardship in this regard.
5. Majority of the women entrepreneurs in Krishna District have got assistance in marketing their products, followed by respondents in Ranga Reddy District and Chittoor District.
6. The same trend is evident in the case of exporting of products by small enterprises promoted by women entrepreneurs in Krishna, Ranga Reddy & Chittoor Districts.
7. About the management consultancy services provided by the Institutions/Agencies to women entrepreneurs, 50 percent of the respondents in Ranga Reddy District were dissatisfied, while it was 60 percent in the case of Chittoor District and 33.34 percent in Krishna District.

8. In the case of Extension Services provided by the Institutions/Agencies, majority of the respondents were happy about the services provided in Krishna District, while in Ranga Reddy the opinion was divided amongst the respondents and it was 40 percent in Chittoor Districts.
9. Majority of the women entrepreneurs maintained contact with other co-participants of the programme in the case of Krishna District, while it was 50 percent in the case of Ranga Reddy District and 40 percent in Chittoor District.
10. The same scenario prevails in the case of Women entrepreneurs in availing Support & Sustaining functions, as it was the case with stimulatory functions. The women entrepreneurs from Krishna District, followed by Ranga Reddy District and Chittoor Districts availed the support and sustaining functions.

Suggestions

1. Systematic women entrepreneurship development holds great promise. The need for developing women entrepreneurship in unquestionable. The greater the emphasis on developing women entrepreneurship, the higher the status and power it attains in its long term economic planning and the more the thrust on development and promotion of women entrepreneurs, the larger the dispersal of economic power within the country.
2. Action in favour of women has been more welfare oriented than development oriented and generally no constructive steps are taken on a large scale to lead women towards self-employment and entrepreneurship. This needs to be changed and the realization is to harness the growth potential of educated unemployed women, is very important.
3. It is important to select and train the right women, it is necessary to take social and economic conditions of women in India into consideration. Women from the lowest strata of society because it is not possible to survive

with their meagre facility income and are, therefore, interested in earning a definite daily income, which is a must for their survival. The second group of women comes from lower middle strata of society, which makes this group interested in small cottage industry where they could remain their own homes and still work. Yet another group hails from a different social pattern and life style. This group is aware of the scope of industrial development in the country. These women are either technically qualified or have years of working experience in various fields. This group is suitable for non-traditional areas in business and industry. Another group of women are those who wanted to become entrepreneurs but could not. They do have the desire and ambition but are neither technically qualified nor have any working experience. Majority of women entrepreneurs belong to this group. These women are generally from the middle income group families and can devote sufficient time for a business enterprise due to reduced family responsibilities.

4. In order to optimize the efforts and cost, and also to ensure better results and performance, scientific selection procedure should be designed. Women entrepreneurs need certain competencies to succeed in business. These competencies can be identified and can also be developed. The purpose of the selection will, therefore, be to test or assess the existing level of these competencies in a women entrepreneur.
5. Potential women entrepreneurs, before they initiate and launch their enterprises, would thoroughly understand the environment under which they will work. This is required because after knowing one's existing levels of competency and the environment, one can plan achieving one's goal.
6. Women entrepreneurs should be made sensitive to the environment and should be helped to identify and select the viable business opportunity. Prospective women entrepreneurs should be helped in developing capabilities

of selecting suitable project, conceiving and formulating it according to their own capabilities and assess its viability. These inputs will enable women entrepreneurs and develop the skills to identify, assess and select the right business opportunity.

7. Before launching a new venture, women entrepreneurs need to study the feasibility of the new product by conducting a market survey. Market survey will help women entrepreneurs to assess the potentiality of the product's life on their own and prepare their preliminary business plans.
8. Developing the individual competencies to run the business in the potential women entrepreneurs are of paramount importance and increases the chances of success. The inputs will help women entrepreneurs to understand the importance and relevance of these competencies and to develop the same through the training.
9. Women entrepreneurs have to monitor and control the production and therefore need technical orientation. She has to apply technology in her entrepreneurial career. Exposure to technology will help in removing the fear of technology found especially amongst women.
10. Appropriate training is the key to a successful programme to develop entrepreneurship among women. Continuous monitoring and improvement of training programmes should eventually spread the cult of entrepreneurship among young women. All this can be achieved in a training environment, especially one in which the woman is distanced from the normal restrictive family environment and is taught to recognize her own psychological needs and express them. Repeated exposure to women who are successfully managing enterprises might encourage some women who are passive now to involve themselves to a greater extent in the enterprises promoted by them.

11. A major area of difficulty for women entrepreneurs is marketing. The long term strategy should in any case be to inculcate marketing skills in women entrepreneurs to enable them to produce for the market. This means that a market survey to select the product should be made part of all training and advice given to expose enterprises to markets and make them responsive to them. Professional marketing expertise is essential to identify marketing channels for the products made by women entrepreneurs.
12. There is a need to revamp the working of District Industries Centres, since the DICs are expected to assist entrepreneurs in getting licenses/clearances from various departments/agencies. It is difficult for women entrepreneurs to liaise with a number of departments/agencies to get the necessary clearances and approvals. The District Industries Centres could play an important role in assisting the women entrepreneurs, so that they need not have to run from pillar to post.

Bibliography

Bibliography

Abdul Hamid. A.M.: Seminar on Small Scale Industries. The Ernakulam District Small Industries Association, Cochin, April, 1970.

Akhori M.M.P.: Self Employment through Entrepreneurship Development Strategies

Akhouri M.M.P. & S.P. Mishra: Entrepreneurship Education: A Conceptual Base, Approach and Methodology, Indian Management, 1990, Vol.29, Nos. 11 & 12, pp.53-65.

Akhouri Vinod Gupta, MMP: Sustaining Entrepreneurship (Seminar Proceedings), Niesbud, 1990.

Akhouri, MMP (1974): Evaluation of Entrepreneurial Motivation training Programme in Assam, SIET Institute, Hyderabad, 1974.

Akohouri MMP: Training for Entrepreneurship and Self Employment, New Delhi, Mittal Publications, 1999, pp.1-12.

Akram.S.: Development of Small Scale Industries in India. The National Small Industries Corporation Ltd. (A Govt. of India undertaking, New Delhi), 1966.

Alexander (1975): Entrepreneurship Development : Need for a Pragmatic Approach, SEDME, 1975, 2(1), 1-8.

Anjaneya Swamy. G: Agricultural Entrepreneurship in India, Chugh Publication, Allahabad, India, 1989.

Anostuck School of Business Management: Seminar on Entrepreneurship, Working papers and Project Proposal for an Entrepreneurial Process, Dartmoth College, 1969.

Anupa Siddhu: Sustainable Entrepreneurship in Communities, Published by Academic Excellence – New Delhi - ISBN-81-88684-82-1.

Ashok Kumar. S.: Entrepreneurship in Small Industry, Discovery Publishing House, 1990.

Assistance. A.I.D.: Small Scale Industries in India. The National Small Industries Corporation Ltd. (A Govt. of

India undertaking, New Delhi), 1966.

B.E.V.N.N. Murthy (1989) Entrepreneurship in Small Towns, Mittal Publications.

Balakrishnan. G: Financing of Small Scale Industries in India, 1950-52, Gokhale Institute of Economics & Politics, Poona, 1961.

Balakrishnan. G: Financing of Small Scale Industries in India (1950-52). Gokhale Institute of Politics & Economics, Poona.

Basu. S.K.: Place and Problems of Small Industries. Mukherjee & Co. Private Ltd. Calcutta, 1957.

Bedapati Mohanty: Economics of small Scale Industries Ashish Publishing House, New Delhi, 1986.

Bengt. Johannison: University Training for Entrepreneurship: Swedish Approaches, Vaxjo University, Sweden Entrepreneurship & Regional Development, Volume.3, Issue-1, January 1991, Pages 67-82.

Bhat (1976): Entrepreneurship in Curricular of Engineering Studies, Young Alliance, 1976, 8(9), 19-21.

Bhat A.R.: Report of the Committee on Legislation for Small Scale Industries, Government of India, 1972.

Bhat R.S.: Report of the Committee on Development of Small Scale and Medium Entrepreneurs, Govt. of India, 1973.

Bolton J.E.: Report of the Committee of Inquiry on Small Firms, Majesty's Stationary office, 1972.

Bose. A.N.: Calcutta and Rural Bengal : Small Sector Symbiosis. Minerva Associates (Publications) Pvt. Ltd., 1978.

Briga Hynes: Entrepreneurship Education and Training Introducing Entrepreneurship into Non-Business Disciplines, Journal of European Industrial Training, MCB UP Ltd. 1996, Vol:20, Issue:8, Page. 10-17.

Chary N.V.N.: Role of District Industries Centre in Promotion of Entrepreneurship – A study of unpublished Doctoral Dissertation, Selected Districts in Andhra Pradesh, Kakatiya University.

Chebbi (1975) V.K.: Stimulating rural entrepreneurial initiatives, SEDME, 1975, 2(i), 59-72.

Chebbi. V.K.: Capital Requirements of Small Industry. Small Industry Extension Training, Hyderabad, 1974.

Chee Peng Lim: The Role of Small Industry in the Malaysian Economy. Faculty of Economics and Admis. University of Malaya, 1975.

Chee Rend Lim Puthucheary & Donald Lee: A Study of Small Entrepreneurs and Entrepreneurial Development Programme in Malaysia, University of Malaysia Press, 1979.

Chee Reng Lim, M.C. Purthucheary & Donald Lee: A study of Small Entrepreneurs and Entrepreneurial Development Program's in Malaysia (An Adipa Research Project) Faculty of Economics and Administration, University of Malaya, Kuala Lumpur, 1978.

Cliffford. M Bauback Baumback's Guide to Entrepreneurship Prentice Hall Inc., 1981.

D.D. Mali: Training for Entrepreneurship and Self Employment, Mittal Publications, New Delhi, ISBN-81-7099-667-8.

D.D. Mali A.R. Baruah & Nisiet Guwahati: Emerging Entrepreneurship in North East India (Third Select Cases). Govt. of India North Eastern Council, Secretariat, Shillong, 1992.

David Silver. A: Entrepreneurial Megabucks. John Wilkey & Sons, New York 1985.

Dhana, L.p.: The Education and Training of Entrepreneurs in Asia, Education – Training, Emerald Group Publishing Limited, Vol. 43, Nov. 8, 2001, pp.405-416 (12).

Dhar & Lydall: The Role of Small Enterprises in Indian Economic Development, Asia Publishing House, Bombay, 1961.

Dhar P.S.: Small Scale Industries, Asia Publishing House, Bombay, 1958.

Dinesh N. Awasthi and Jose Sebastian: Idib.1996, p.116.

Elizabet Henessy: The Entrepreneurs, Scope Books, 1980.

Eugene Stalley & Richard Morse: Modern Small Industries for Developing Countries. Mc Graw Hills Book Co. New York, 1965.

FASSII (1976): Growth of Entrepreneurship in backward Areas, FASII Bulletin, 1976, 15(5) 7-8 &12.

Gaikwad, V.R., H.Gor, U. Pareek, T.V. Rao and B.G.Sah: An Interview Schedule to Measure Entrepreneurial Behaviours, 11 M, Ahmedabad, 1974.

Gaikwad, V.R., H.Gor, U. Pareek, T.V. Rao, H.C. Sah, B.G. Sah and Mc.Shetty: Entrepreneurship Development Programmes : An Evaluation, Indian Institute of Management, Ahmedabad, 1974.

Gangadhar Rao. N: Entrepreneurship and Growth of Enterprise in Industrial Estates. Deep & Deep publications, New Delhi, 1986.

Gokarn (1973): The Making of Successful Small Scale Entrepreneur, Indian Manager, 1973, 4(1), 51-58.

Gopi. T: Promotion of Small Entrepreneurship in Andhra Pradesh – A comparative study, unpublished Doctoral Dissertation, Kakatiya University, 2005.

Gorden B. Baty: Entrepreneurship playing to win, Prentice Hall, Inc., 1979.

Gordon B. Baty: Entrepreneurship for the Eighties. Reston Publishing Co., 1981.

Guha A.C: Report of the working group on Small Scale Sector, Administrative Reforms Commission Government of India, 1968.

Habibur Rahman .AHM: Entrepreneurship and Small Enterprise development in Bangladesh. Bureau of Business Research, University of Dacca, 1979.

Hadimani. R.N.: Dynamics of Industrial Entrepreneurship. Ashish Publishing House, New Delhi, 1985.

Honstadt: Entrepreneurship. Lord Publishing's, New Delhi, 1985.

Hoover: Overseas Economic Operations – Report to the

Congress, U.C. Commiss9ion on Organization of the Executive Branch of the Government, 1955.

Ichiro Oshikawa & Kenzo Ototake: Outline of Policy for Smaller Enterprises, Japanese Experience. Asian Productivity Organisation, August, 1969.

Inderjit Singh & Gupta, N.S.: Financing of Small Industry, S. Chand & Co. Ltd., New Delhi, 1973.

Inter – Institutional Group of Bihar, 1974: Entrepreneurial Development Programme for Bihar, Patna, 1974.

Jain O.P.: Small Industry Exports – A Study into Promotional Techniques, S. Chand & Co. 1971.

James Curran and John Stanworth: Education and Training for Enterprise: Problems of Classification, Evaluation, Policy and Research, International Small Business Journal, SAGE Publications, Vol.7, No.2, 1989, p.11-22.

James J. & Berna S.J.: Industrial Entrepreneurship in Madras State. Asia Publishing House, Madras, 1960.

James T. McCory: Small Industry in a North Indian Town, Ministry of Commerce & Industry.

Jams J Berna (1960): Industrial Entrepreneurship in Madras State, Asia publishing House, 1960.

Jeanne Hallday Coughlin & Andrew R. Thomas: The Rise of Women Entrepreneurs, People, processes, and Global trends, Published by Quorum Books, West Port London. ISBN-1-56720-462-7 (2002).

Jeffrey. S. Hornsby, Douglas W. Naffizer, Donald, F. Kuratko, & Ray V. Montagno: An Interactive Model of the Corporate Entrepreneurship Process, Journal Entrepreneurship: Theory and Practice, Vol.17, 1993.

K.L. Sharma (1973): Growth of small sale entrepreneurship in India ; theoretical frame of Analysis, inter discipline 1973, (3), 7-108.

Karve: Report of Village and Small Scale Industries (Second Five Year Plan) Committee, Government of India, 1955.

Kilby, (1971): Entrepreneurship and Economic Development, Free Press, New York, 1971.

Konives (1974):What Are Entrepreneur Made of? Chemical technology, 1974, 4 (12), 716-721.

Krishna Swamy K.S.: Seminar on Financing of Small Scale Industries in India, Reserve Bank of India, 1965.

Krishna Swamy K.S.: Seminar on Financing of Small Scale Industries in India, Reserve Bank of India, 1965.

Krishnalal Sharma: Entrepreneurial Performance in Role Perspective. Abhinav Publication, New Delhi, 1975.

Kulakarni, P.R.:Entrepreneurship Development: Role of the Government and Institutional Agencies, Southern Economist, 1999, Vol.38, No.8, pp.12-14.

Kuratko, Donald. F:The Emergence of Entrepreneurship Education: Development, Trends and Challenges, Entrepreneurship Theory and Practice, Blackwell, Publishing, Vol.29, No.5, Sept. 2005, pp.577-598 (22).

Leon V Chico: Small Enterprise and Entrepreneurship Development in Eleven Asian Pacific Countries. Tochnonet Asia and Singapore, 1983.

Lift (1974): Why Entrepreneurs succeed, Journal of General management, 1974, 1(2), 77-93.

Liles (1974): Who are the entrepreneurs? MSU Business Topics, 1974, 22(1), 5-14.

M. Gangadhara Rao (1992): Entrepreneurship and Entrepreneurial Development, Kanishka Publishing House, New Delhi, ISBN-81-85475-43-1

M.A. Khan:Entrepreneurial Development Programmes in India, Kanishka Publishing House, New Delhi, ISBN-81-85-475-31-8 (1992).

Malcom Harper Tan Thasam Scan: Small Enterprises in Developing Countries: Case studies and conclusions. Intermediate Technology Publications Ltd., London, 1979.

Malgarkar P.D. (1974): Training for Entrepreneurial Development; review and approach occasional paper No.51 Training Division, Dept. of Personnel and Administrative Reform, New Delhi, 1974.

Mandy (1973): Motives, Modernity and Entrepreneurial

Competence, Journal of Social Psychology, 1973, 91(I Half) 127-136.

Mark Casson: The Entrepreneur an Economic Theory. Martin Robertson, 1982.

McClelland, D.C.: Achievement Motive, Irving Publishers, New York, 1976.

McClelland, DC & Winter David G: Motivating Economic Achievement, Free Press, New York, 1971.

Michael J.C. Martin: Managing Technological Innovation and Entrepreneurship. Reston Publishing Company Inc. Reston, Virginia, 1984.

Ministry of Industrial Development, 1975: Report of the Committee on Development of small and medium Entrepreneurs, India investment Centre, 1975.

Muthaiah, B.C. & M. Loganathan: Psychosocial Factors influencing Entrepreneurship in Rural Areas, Journal of Rural Development, Vol.9, No.1, 1990, pp.237-38.

Nafees Baig & Mohd. Asif Ali Khan: Entrepreneurship and Business Environment. Ashish Publishing House, New Delhi, 1990.

Nafziger (1975): Entrepreneurship in India, Political Science Quarterly, 1975, LXXX(4), P.558-573.

Nafziger (1975): Class, Caste and Community of South Indian industrialists: An examination of Horatio-Alger Model, the Journal of development studies, 1975, 11(2), 131-148.

Nagendra P. Singh: Entrepreneurship Development (Theory & Practice) Inter Cultural Foundation for Development Management, Government of India Press, Delhi, 1985.

Nanjundan .S Robinson .H.E. & Eugene Staley: Economic Research for Small Industry Development. Asia Publishing House, Madras, 1962.

Narendra S. Bisht and Pamila K. Sharma: Entrepreneurship Expectations and Experience, Himalaya Publication House, New Delhi, 1991.

Narendra S. Bisht, Ramesh C. Misra & Anil K. Srivastava (1989): Entrepreneurship Reflections and Investigations,

Published by Chugh Publications, Allahabad. ISBN-81-85076-62-6

Natarajan. K and M. Jayarathnam: Entrepreneurship: A Means to Women Development, Khadi Gramodyog, Vol.37, No.12, 1991, pp.357-360.

Neal, E.,: Thornberry Corporate Entrepreneurship: Teaching Managers to be Entrepreneurs, Journal of Management Development, MCB UP Ltd. 2003, Vol.22, Issue:4, Page 329-344.

Newalker (1971): Creating Environment for Entrepreneurship, Productivity, 1971, 12(1), 35-38.

Pareek H.S.: Financing of Small Industries in Developing Economy, National Publishing Economy House, 1978.

Patel V.G.: Entrepreneurial and Economic Profile of a Small Scale Unit, Gujarat Industries Corporation Ahmedabad, 1975.

Patel. V.V.: Entrepreneurial and Economic Profile of a Small Scale Unit. Gujarat Industries Corporation, Ahmedabad, 1975.

Pathak H.H.: Problem of Small Scale Entrepreneurs. Industrial Development Bank of India, 1975.

Pathak H.N.: Problems of Small Scale Entrepreneurs, Industrial Development Bank of India, Bombay.

Pathak H.N. (1975) : Problems of Small Scale Entrepreneurs: Report on a study based in Gujarat, Industrial Development Bank of India, 1975.

Patil, V.G., A. Trivedi & H.C. Rawal: How to successfully fail in EDPs, Occasional Papers, entrepreneurship Development institute of India, Ahmedabad, 1984.

Patrick R. Liles (1974): New Business Venture and entrepreneur, Richard D. Irwin, 1974.

Patwardhan (1976): What banks expect from the Small Scale Industries, Industrial Times, 1976, 18(8), 27-31.

Peter Kilby:Entrepreneurship and Economic Development. The Free Press, New York, 1978.

Peter Kilby:Entrepreneurship and Economic Development.

The Free Press, New York, 1971.

Prabath S.V.: Entrepreneurship Development in India: A Review, SEDME, 1996, Vol.XXX, No.3, pp.1-5.

Rabindra N. Kanungo (1998): Entrepreneurship and Innovation Models for Development, Sage Publications, New Delhi.

Radhakrishnan. R: Evaluation of Entrepreneurship Development Programme in Tamil Nadu, Unpublished Doctoral Dissertation, Kakatiya University, 1994.

Rajinder Sachar: Report of the High Powered Expert Committee on Companies & MRTP Acts, Government of India.

Ram K. Vepa: Small Industry development programme. Indian Institute of Public Administration, New Delhi, 1983.

Ram P.N.: Entrepreneurship in Education Main Stream, The Hindu, 1998.

Ram Sagar Singh: Rural elite Entrepreneurship and Social Change. Rawat Publication, 1985.

Ramakrishna K.T.: Finance for Small Scale Industry in India, Asia Publishing House, Bombay.

Ramakrishna. P : New Entrepreneurship in Small Scale Industry in Delhi. Economic and Scientific Research Foundation, New Delhi, 1975.

Ramanujan, KNR: Report of the Committee on Delayed Payments to Small Scale Units, Reserve Bank of India, Bombay.

Rao T.V. (1975): Development of an Entrepreneur: A Behaviourist model, SEDME, 1975, 1(4), 325-343.

Rao T.V., Udai Pareek: Developing Entrepreneurship; A Handbook of Learning Systems, Delhi, 1978

Rao. B.S.V.: A Multi Dimensional Approach to Entrepreneurship Significance of Training and other inputs" SEDME, 1975, Vol.1, No.4, pp.75-87.

Rathore, B.S., D.D.Sharma & S.K. Dhanuja: Impact of Various Schemes on Technical Entrepreneurs, HRD

Times, 1998.

Ravi Prakash. S : Financing of Small Scale Industries in Madras City, Unpublished Doctoral Dissertation, University of Poona, 1982.

Renuka: Development of Women Entrepreneurship – A Case Study of Kurnool District in Andhra Pradesh, unpublished Doctoral Dissertation, Sri Krishna Devaraya University, Anantapur, 2006.

Richard Scarze and Robert Goffee: The Entrepreneurship Middle Class. Gorom Helm London's, Canberra, 1982.

Robert Ronstadt. C : Enterpreneurship, Lord Publishing, Madras, 1984.

Ronade. S.P.: Entrepreneurship Development Model for 21st Century: A Short Note, SEDME, 1996, Vol.XXIII, No.2, PP.47-48.

Rondinelli &Johnson (1975): Decision Making Managerial capacity and Development : An entrepreneurial approach to planning, African Administrative Studies, 1975, (13), 105-118.

Sadhad. H: The Role of Entrepreneur in Backward Area, New Delhi: Daya Publishing House, 1989.

Sahney. M: "Women Entrepreneurship on the G O", Financial Express, 1989, Oct. 14, p.7.

Saini J.S., & B.S. Bhatia: Impact of Entrepreneurship Development programmes, Journal of Entrepreneurship Development, 1996, pp.23-27.

Samiuddin (1989): Entrepreneurship Development in India, Mittal Publications, New Delhi ISBN-81-7099-115-3.

Sarah L.Jack, Alistair. R, Anderson : Entrepreneurship Education within the Enterprise Culture: Producing Reflective Practitioners, International journal of Entrepreneurial Behaviour 7 Research, 125, McB UP Ltd., 1999, Vol : 5, Issue: 3 p.110.

Satya Narayana Chary.T: Venture Capital, Concepts & Applications, MacMillan, 2005.

Sharma: Enterpreneurial Performance in Role Perspective.

Abhinav Publications, New Delhi, 1975.

Sharma (1975): Stimulation of Entrepreneurship in less developed areas, some Indian experiences, SEDME, 1975, 1(4), 345-363.

Sharma K.L. (1975): Entrepreneurial Performance in Role Perspective, Abhinav Publications, New Delhi, 1975.

Sharma R.A.: Enterpreneurial Change in India Industry, Sterling Publishers Pvt. Ltd., 1980.

Sharma R.A.: Entrepreneurial performance in Indian industry. Inter India publication, New Delhi, 1985.

Sharma R.A.: Enterpreneurial performance in India Industry. Inter India Publication, D 17, Raja Garden Extn., New Delhi, 1985.

Sharma SVS (1979): Small Entrepreneurial Development in Some Asian Countries, Light and Life publishers, New Delhi, 1979.

Shiva Ramu .S: Entrepreneurship and Enterprise Growth. Seema Publications, 1985.

Shyam Sunder. Chitta: Role of SIDBI in Entrepreneurship Development of Andhra Pradesh, Doctoral Dissertation Kakatiya University, 2005.

SIET (1974): Socio-Psychological factor influencing the adoption of the innovation of starting a small industry unit : A research study, SIET Institute, Hyderabad, 1974.

Singh P.N.: Development Entrepreneurship for Economic Growth. Vikas Publishing, 1986.

Singh, NP & Kiran Kumar (1971): Motivational Structure Underlying Entrepreneurship Behaviourometric, 1971, 1(2), 89-98.

Sinha, SLN: Sickness of Industrial Units, Institute of Financial Management & Research, Madras, 1977.

Srivastava. A.K., R.C. Mishra & N.S. Bisht : Developing Entrepreneurship: A Strategic Layout, Man and Development, SEDME, 1988, Vol.10, No.3, pp.117-124.

Subarana M.C.: Entrepreneurial Development Programme for Bihar. Bholanath Industries, Patna, 1974.

Suresh, B.H.: Industrial Entrepreneurship in Karnataka – A Case Study of Small Scale Industrial Units in Mysore District, Unpublished Ph.D. thesis submitted to university of Mysore, 1992.

Tandon (1975): Environment and Entrepreneur, Chug Publication, 1975.

Thanulingam Nadar .N: Small Scale Industry Interrelationship with Large Scale Industry. Rainbow Publication Coimbatore, 1985.

Thomas N. Garavan & Barra O'Cinneide: Entrepreneurship Education and Training Programme. A Review and Evaluation – Part-I, Journal of European Industrial Training, MCB UP Ltd. 1994, Vol.18, Issue:8, Page: 3-12.

Timmons (1975): Guided Entrepreneurship, Business, Horizons, 1975, 18(6), 49-52.

Uplonkar (1972): A Study of Self-employed Industrial Entrepreneurs, the Indian Journal of Social Work, 1977, 38(2), 137-147.

Van der Veen: A Study of Small Industries in Gujarat State, Occasional Paper No.65, Department of Agricultural Economics, Cornell University.

Van Der Veen (1976): Commercial Orientation of Industrial Entrepreneurs in India, Economic and Political Weekly, 1976,11(35), M.91-94.

Vardan (1971): Development of Ancillaries and Entrepreneurial Skills, Integrated Managements, 1971, 61,10-14.

Venkat Rao (1975): A Multi-dimensional approach to development of entrepreneurship : Significance of training and other inputs, SEDME, 1975, 1(4), 285-300.

Verma M.K.: Government – Institute – Industry Partnership, EDII, Ahmedabad, 1996.

Vinayshil Gautam (1979): Enterprise and Society : A Study of Some aspects of Entrepreneurship and Management in India, Concept Publishing, 1979.

Vinod K. Agarwal (1975): Initiative Enterprise and

Economic choices in India : A Study of the Patterns of Entrepreneurship, Munshiram Manoharlal, 1975

Webster (1977): Entrepreneurs and Ventures – An attempt at classification and clarification. Academy of Management review, 1977, 2(1), 54-61.

William Copulsky Herbert .W Mc Nutty: Entrepreneurship and the Corporation. A American Management Association, 1974.

William Naumes: The Entrepreneurial Manager in the Small Business. Addison Wesley publishing company, London, 1978.

Zafar Ataf: Pakistani Entrepreneurship. IBD Publishing and Distribution, 1984.

Index

Index

A
A.P State Financial Corporation (APSFC), 97
Achievement Motivation Training (AMT), 85
Adequacy of Skills to Impart Training, 131
Adverse Effects of Risk Bearing, 80
All India Organisation of Employers (AIOE), 13
Amostuck School of Business Management (1969), 40
Andhra Pradesh Industrial Infrastructure Corporation, 150
Awareness Building and Networking, 90

B
Bank of India's Priyadarshini Yojana, 97
Barriers Faced by Women Entrepreneurs, 74
Beijing Declaration (1995), 58

C
Central Institute of Tool Design (CITD), 38
Central Social Welfare Board (CSWB), 118
Centre for Entrepreneurship Development (CED), 85
Characteristics of Entrepreneurs, 6
Clientele Satisfaction of Stimulatory Functions, 175
Clientele Satisfaction of Support and Sustaining Functions, 176
Committee of Development of Small and Medium Enterprises (1975), 21
Concept and Status of Women Entrepreneurs, 54
Concept of Entrepreneurship, 1
Convention on Elimination of All Forms of Discrimination against Women (CEDAW), 58
Convention on the Rights of the Child (CRC), 73
Cost Benefit Analysis, 134

D
David McClelland, 6

Decade for Women (1975-85), 12
Development Agencies in Andhra Pradesh, 149
District Industries Centre (DIC), 141
District Legal Service Authority (DLSA), 114
Dowry Prohibition Act (DPA), 111

E

Economic Empowerment of Women, 61
Effective Implementation of Women Related Legislations, 111
Eleventh Five Year Plan (2007-12) on Women Empowerment, 101
Eleventh Plan Schemes, 116
Employers Federation of India (EFI), 13
Enterprise Establishment and Management, 95
Entrepreneurial Attitude Orientation, 178
Entrepreneurial Behavioural Skills & Competency Development, 95
Entrepreneurial Development Programme (EDP), 100
Entrepreneurship and Economic Development, 2
Entrepreneurship and Social Organisation, 3
Entrepreneurship Development in India, 10
Entrepreneurship Development Programme (EDP), 13, 53, 84, 85
Entrepreneurship Training Programmes, 31
Entrepreneurship: Characteristics and Motivation, 25
Entrepreneurship: Selection and Training, 27

F

Federation of Andhra Pradesh Chamber of Commerce & Industry (Women Wing), 152
Findings Regarding Stimulatory Functions, 179
Findings Regarding Support and Sustaining Functions, 183
Functions and Role of

Women Entrepreneurs, 75
Functions of Entrepreneurship, 4

G
Gender and Development Approach (GAD), 49
Gender Development Indices (GDI), 68
Gender Mainstreaming and Strengthening Delivery Mechanisms, 113
Group Level Pattern Function, 4
Guidance of Women Entrepreneurs, 130
Gujarat Industrial Investment Corporation (GIIC), 84

H
High Achievement Function, 5
Hindu Succession (Amendment) Act 2005, 111
Hindu Succession Act (1956), 102
Homes and Homesteads for Poor Women, 107

I
Identification and Selection of Potential Women Entrepreneurs, 91
Identification and Selection of Product, 94
Identification of Potential Women Entrepreneurs, 128
Impact of Globalisation and Eleventh Plan Strategy, 106
Industrial Credit and Investment Corporation of India (ICICI), 85
Industrial Development Bank of India (IDBI), 14, 85
Industrial Financial Corporation of India (IFCI), 85
Infant Mortality Rate (IMR), 64
Innovation Function, 4
Input-completing and Gap Filling Function, 5
Institute for Design and of Electrical Measuring
Instruments (IDEMI), 38, 125
Institutional Support for Entrepreneurship, 28
Inter-agency Co-operation, 124
Inter-Institutional Group of

Bihar (1974), 20
International Conference on Population and Development, 73

J

James Berna, 20
James Curran, 32
Jeanne Halladay, 29

K

K.L. Sharma, 24
Khadi and Village Industries Commission (KVIC), 124, 142

L

Lack of Working Capital, 74
Land Rights for Women, 106
Leadership Function, 4

M

Mahila Udyam Nidhi (MUN) Scheme, 99
Mahila Vikas Nidhi (MVN) Scheme, 99
Married Women's Property Act (1874), 102
Maternal Mortality Rate (MMR), 64
McClelland, 21
Methodology of Training, 126
Mexico Plan of Action (1975), 58
Micro Credit Programme, 84
Models of Entrepreneurship Development, 40
Motivation for Entrepreneurship among Women, 16
Motivation of Women Entrepreneurs, 127
Motivational Climate of Institutions/Agencies, 172

N

Nairobi Forward Looking Strategies (1985), 58
National Alliance of Young Entrepreneurs (NAYE), 12
National Commission for Women (NCW), 113
National Institute for Entrepreneurship and Small Business Development (NIESBUD), 38, 86
National Institute of Small Industry Extension Training (NISIET), 12
National Institute of Small Industry Extension, 139
National Plan of Action for

Children 2005, 102
National Policy for the Empowerment of Women, 2001, 57
National Policy on Women 2001, 102
National Population Policy 2000, 64
National Science and Technology Entrepreneurship Development Board (NSTDB), 13
National Small Industries Corporation (NSIC), 124, 143
New Economic Policy (NEP), 15
Norwegian Agency for International Development (NORAD), 14

O

Organisation Building Function, 5
Over-dependence on Intermediaries, 78

P

Personal Entrepreneurial Competencies (PECs), 93
Personal Risk Taking in Select Districts, 168
Politico-legal Empowerment of Women, 60
Post-training Contact of Institutions, 137
Pre-investment Analysis, 135
Preliminary Analysis of Alternatives, 135
Preparation of Feasibility Report, 133
Preparation of Project Plan, 94
Pre-requisites of Successful Entrepreneurship, 165
Problems of Women Entrepreneurs, 77
Processes of Entrepreneurship Development, 18
Project Design and Network Analysis, 133
Protection of Women from Domestic Violence Act, (2005), 102, 111

R

Rashtriya Mahila Kosh, 117
Rise of Women Entrepreneurs, 29
Role of Gender in Economic Development, 53
Role of Institutions in

Providing Financial Assistance, 157
Role of Multinational Corporations (MNCs), 82
Role of Non-governmental Organisations (NGOs), 83

S
Scarcity of Raw Materials, 78
Scheme of Interest Subsidy for Women Entrepreneurs, 98
Science and Technology Entrepreneurial Parks (STEPs), 14
Selection of Potential Women Entrepreneurs, 129
Selection of Tools and Techniques, 93
Self-employed Women's Association (SEWA), 83
Sensitization Workshops and Networking, 91
Small Enterprise Management Assistance Programme (SEMA), 16
Small Industries Development Bank of India (SIDBI), 85, 144
Small Industries Development Organization (SIDO), 124
Small Industries Service Institute (SISI), 85, 143
Small Industry Development Bank of India's (SIDBI) Scheme of Assistance for Women Entrepreneurs, 97
Small Industry Development Organisation (SIDCO), 12
Social Empowerment of Women, 63
Social, Political and Economic Functions, 6
Socio-Cultural Barriers, 75
Standing Conference of Public Enterprises (SCOPE), 13
State Bank of India's (SBI) Stree Shakti Package, 100
State Financial Corporations (SFC), 141
Status Withdrawal Function, 5
Strategies for Developing Women Entrepreneurship, 55

T

Technical Consultancy Organisations (TCOs), 85
Techno Economic Analysis, 133
The National Commission for Women, 58
Training and Employment Programme, 116
Training and Motivating of Women Entrepreneurs, 123
Tripartite Committee, 161

U

Uplaonkar, 24

V

Vinayshil Gautam, 20
Vinod Agarwal, 19

W

Women Empowerment and Livelihood Project, 117
Women Entrepreneurship Development (WED) Programme, 87
Women Entrepreneurship in India, 12
Women in Agriculture, 105
Women in the Unorganized Sector, 105
Women's Enterprises Management Training Outreach Programme (WEMTOP), 16